HISTORY OF THE WORLD

THE ISLAMIC WORLD: FROM ITS ORIGINS TO THE 16TH CENTURY

RAINTREE
STECK-VAUGHN
PUBLISHERS
The Steck-Vaughn Company

Austin, Texas

This book has been reviewed for accuracy by
Christopher S. Taylor, Drew University

Il Mondo dell'Islam ©1991 by Editoriale Jaca Book, Milan

English translation copyright ©1994 by Steck-Vaughn Company

All rights reserved. No part of the material protected by this copyright may be reproduced or utilized in any form or by any means, electronic or mechanical, including photocopying, recording, or by any information storage and retrieval system, without permission in writing from the copyright owner. Requests for permission to make copies of any part of the work should be mailed to: Copyright Permissions, Steck-Vaughn Company, P.O. Box 26015, Austin, TX 78755

Italian text by Monica Colombo
Illustrations for cover and interior by Giacinto Gaudenzi and Giorgio Bacchin
English translation by Pamela Swinglehurst

Cover Design by Cath Polito

Raintree Steck-Vaughn Editorial
Helene Resky: Editor

Electronic Production
Management by Design

Printed and bound in the United States of America

1 2 3 4 5 6 7 8 9 0 LB 98 97 96 95 94

Library of Congress Cataloging-in-Publication Data
Colombo, Monica
 [Mondo dell'Islam. English]
 The Islamic World / written by Monica Colombo.
 p. cm. — [History of the World]
 ISBN 0-8114-3328-5
 1. Islamic Empire – Juvenile literature. 2. Civilization, Islamic – Juvenile literature.
I. Title. II. Series.

 DS38.3.C6513 1994
 909'.097671 – dc20
                                                   93-31449
                                                   CIP
                                                   AC

TABLE OF CONTENTS

Muslim Expansion to the End of the 11th Century	4
The Arabs Before Islam	6
Muhammad and the Birth of Islam	8
The Early Islamic Conquests and the Formation of the Muslim Empire	10
The Sunnis and the Shi'ites	12
The Umayyad Empire	14
Abbasids Institutions, Economy, and Social Structure	16
The Abbasids – A Blending of Many Different Peoples	18
Artistic Splendor and Philosophy	20
The Army and the Fleet	22
Iran and Islam	24
Trade and Trade Routes	26
Agricultural Production and Farming Techniques	28
Islamic Egypt	30
The Fatimids and Saladin	32
The Seljuk Turks	34
Islamic Spain	36
The Maghrib Before the Almoravids	38
The Maghrib: The Almoravids and the Almohads	40
The Impact of the Mongols on the Muslim World	42
Tamerlane	44
The Mamluks	46
The Ottomans	48
The Fall of Constantinople and the Splendor of Istanbul	50
Ottoman Supremacy in the Islamic World	52
The Age of Suleiman the Magnificent	54
Islam in India	56
Islam in Africa South of the Sahara	59
The Larger Islamic World	61
The Extent of Islam at the End of the 16th Century	63
Glossary	64
Index	66

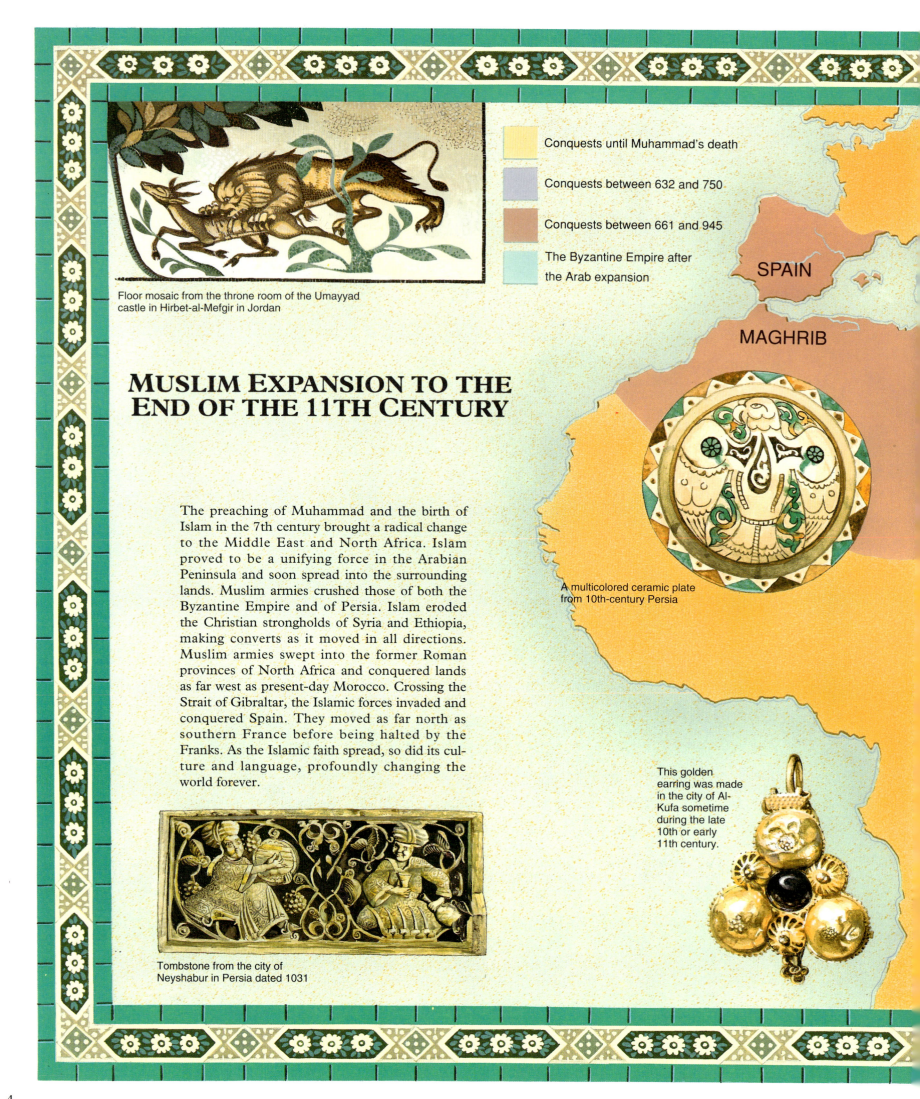

Floor mosaic from the throne room of the Umayyad castle in Hirbet-al-Mefgir in Jordan

- Conquests until Muhammad's death
- Conquests between 632 and 750
- Conquests between 661 and 945
- The Byzantine Empire after the Arab expansion

MUSLIM EXPANSION TO THE END OF THE 11TH CENTURY

The preaching of Muhammad and the birth of Islam in the 7th century brought a radical change to the Middle East and North Africa. Islam proved to be a unifying force in the Arabian Peninsula and soon spread into the surrounding lands. Muslim armies crushed those of both the Byzantine Empire and of Persia. Islam eroded the Christian strongholds of Syria and Ethiopia, making converts as it moved in all directions. Muslim armies swept into the former Roman provinces of North Africa and conquered lands as far west as present-day Morocco. Crossing the Strait of Gibraltar, the Islamic forces invaded and conquered Spain. They moved as far north as southern France before being halted by the Franks. As the Islamic faith spread, so did its culture and language, profoundly changing the world forever.

A multicolored ceramic plate from 10th-century Persia

Tombstone from the city of Neyshabur in Persia dated 1031

This golden earring was made in the city of Al-Kufa sometime during the late 10th or early 11th century.

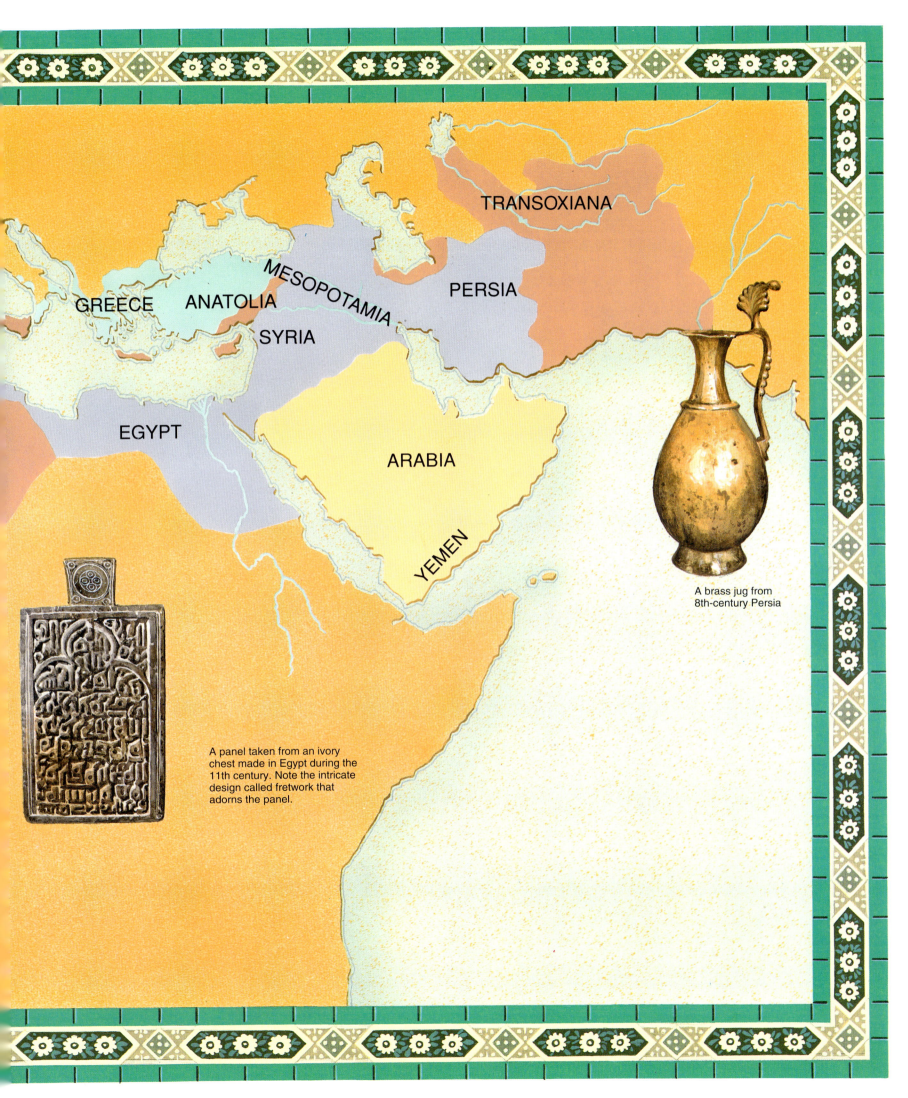

A brass jug from 8th-century Persia

A panel taken from an ivory chest made in Egypt during the 11th century. Note the intricate design called fretwork that adorns the panel.

THE ARABS BEFORE ISLAM

The floor plan above is for the Temple of Baal in Palmyra. Built in A.D. 130, the temple shows the influence of the Roman-Hellenistic style common in that era. Palmyra had already lost some of its independence and was part of the Roman Empire.

In pre-Islamic days there were four major travel routes from southern Arabia to the major commercial centers of the Middle East. One route connected northern Yemen with central Arabia. Another went from Yemen to the cities along the Euphrates River. A third stretched into Syria, and a fourth was a direct route between the city of Yathrib (later Medina) and Petra.

This bust of Aphrodite was carved in the first century A.D. in Yemen. The bust of a Roman goddess in southern Arabia shows how far the influence of Rome had spread.

An inscription in ancient South Arabian characters. Ruins of temples and a great dam are all that is left of the ancient civilizations of southern Arabia.

This small statue of a Himyarite man was made out of alabaster in either the 5th or 6th century A.D. The Himyarites were one of the last settled tribes of southern Yemen to be conquered by Islamic warriors.

The Arabian Peninsula has always been sparsely populated, especially when compared to the nearby areas of Egypt and Mesopotamia. The physical features of the peninsula and its strategic location have strongly influenced the cultures of the peoples inhabiting it. These cultures have varied greatly but have shared some characteristics, such as mobility and a strong interest in trade.

The peninsula was probably penetrated by tribes from Mesopotamia around 1000 B.C., but there is some evidence that people lived in the peninsula long before that. The domestication of the camel 5,000 years ago made it possible for nomadic tribes to travel throughout Arabia. The camel is an excellent beast of burden, able to travel long distances with little water. It is an ideal means of transportation for a desert civilization.

Among the earliest cultures of the peninsula were those of the Thamud, the Nabataens of Petra, the Palmyrenes, and the cultures of the two ancient kingdoms of Hira and Ghassan. The people of these early cultures eventually came under the control of either the Persian or Byzantine empires.

The Thamud never built a strong, centralized government. From the evidence they left behind, they were a nomadic, tribal people devoted to raising animals. Their decline was hastened by the rise of the Nabataean civilization.

The Nabataeans succeeded in establishing a well-organized state centered around the city of Petra. They developed into a commercial power that was well known throughout the Mediterranean area. During the Hellenistic Age, Petra became a powerful city.

The Nabataean civilization was strongly influenced by the Ptolemaic society of Egypt and by the Seleucid dynasty of Asia Minor. The Nabataeans kept their independence until the 2nd century A.D., when the Roman emperor Trajan conquered them and annexed their lands to the Roman Empire.

Palmyra remained relatively independent after the Nabataeans came under Roman control. Palmyra, situated between the Roman Empire and the Parthian Empire in eastern Asia, served as a buffer state between the Romans and the

Yemeni region: The cities are strongholds in the mountain foothills. Peasants and shepherds live in the valleys and plains. In the foreground is an incense tree. The incense and myrrh cultivated in this region were used in religious ceremonies, funeral rites, the preparation of medicines, and in perfumes and cosmetics.

Pre-Islamic Arabic Poetry

Among the main themes of pre-Islamic Arabic poetry are transient love, valor in battle, and the detailed contemplation of nature. These poetic compositions, which were passed down orally by traveling poets, tell us a lot about the life of the nomads and the settled populations of central Arabia. It was also by virtue of this vast heritage that the Arabic language, with its wealth of imagery, became an important unifying factor in the scattered tribal world.

Parthians. However, the Palmyrenes, under Queen Zenobia, revolted against Roman influence. In A.D. 272, the Roman emperor Aurelian had the city sacked and destroyed.

Much less is known about the history of the tribes inhabiting the vast desert regions of central Arabia. These tribes were known as Bedouins, and they were fierce warriors and shrewd traders. They controlled important channels of commerce between the Nabataeans, the Palmyrenes in the north, and the southern coastal areas of Arabia. Despite the blood ties of the Bedouin tribes, they often battled one another.

Some of the tribes established cities. The most important of these cities was Mecca, which, because of its central location along the trade routes, became wealthy and powerful. Eventually Mecca controlled most of the caravan trade throughout the peninsula. Mecca was also an important religious center. Many idols, including a holy black stone, were kept in Mecca in a religious sanctuary called the Ka'aba. Many pilgrims came to Mecca in order to venerate their gods.

The southern coastal areas of Arabia are very different from the deserts of the vast central plateaus. The southern part of the peninsula has good rainfall, fertile land, and a pleasant climate. The people of these southern lands, also known as Yemen, were ideally placed to control commerce between Africa and Asia.

During ancient times, Yemen also became a center for the production and export of spices and expensive fragrances, such as frankincense and myrrh. The area remained relatively free from outside influence until it was invaded by the Abyssinians from East Africa during the 6th century A.D.

The decline of southern Arabia was brought on in part by a drop in demand for the fragrances produced in the region. The fragrances, used in cremation ceremonies, were not used by the growing Christian population. All that is left today of the ancient civilizations that flourished in southern Arabia are the ruins of a large dam that once held back reservoirs of rainwater, the remains of temples used for religious services, and a great number of stone inscriptions.

MUHAMMAD AND THE BIRTH OF ISLAM

A small Indian *minbar*, or raised platform, from which an imam (spiritual leader) leads the faithful in understanding the word of God

A large Egyptian *minbar*, once in use in the mosque of the Sultan Qaytbay (1468-1496)

The *mihrab* is a niche found in every mosque. It indicates the direction of Mecca, the city on the Arabian Peninsula toward which all Muslims face when praying. This *mihrab* is in the Mosque of the Prophet in Medina.

Muhammad was born into the powerful Quraysh tribe in Mecca around the year A.D. 570. His parents died when he was an infant, and he was brought up first by his grandfather and then by his uncle, Abu Talib.

Muhammad went into the trading business when he became an adult. As a trader, Muhammad was in contact with Arab travelers returning from many lands. This gave him the opportunity to learn about different customs and religions.

When he was about 29 years old, Muhammad married Khadija, a wealthy Meccan widow and businesswoman for whom he worked. Khadija was the first person to learn about his prophetic visions and the first to believe in his divine inspiration. She remained his constant supporter for the rest of her life.

The manner in which the revelations came to Muhammad is described in Hadith, collections of traditions relating to the utterances and deeds of the Prophet. Muhammad was already a grown man who had never opposed the pagan beliefs of the Meccan tribes when the revelations began.

One day when Muhammad was spending a period of religious meditation alone in a cave in the hills around Mecca, the angel Gabriel appeared to him in a vision. "Recite," the angel said. This word is the very first word revealed to Muhammad. The angel told Muhammad that he was to preach in the name of Allah, the one and only God. From that moment on, Muhammad received what every Muslim believes were true messages from God. Muhammad began to spread the word of this revelation publicly after several years.

Muhammad's preaching represented a clear challenge to the traditional religious rites of pagan society. Most of the Meccan aristocracy met Muhammad's preaching with hostility. At first the Prophet's preaching attracted converts primarily from the lowest ranks of Mecca's inhabitants, and this may have caused the ruling class to fear social unrest, in addition to the obvious economic threat to Mecca as a pilgrimage center.

In 622, Muhammad had to flee Mecca and emigrate to the city of Yathrib, which is now known as Medina, after his uncle and protector Abu Talib died. It is from the year of Muhammad's flight to Medina that Muslims date the beginning of the Islamic calendar. The flight itself is called the Hijra.

Muhammad was able to bring peace to the warring factions in Medina and was then able to preach freely and to create a large group of followers. The rites and first laws of Islam were established in accordance with Muhammad's instructions. He thus became both a religious and political leader. Within a short time the Prophet had gathered so many followers that he could defy the Meccans. In 630 he returned in triumph to his native city.

Muhammad died in 632, but the number of believers in his preaching continued to spread throughout Arabia. Islam, which means "submission (to the will of God)," had been created. The Muslims, "those who have submitted," were its faithful.

The Five Pillars of Islam

The Islamic faith has five basic precepts that every Muslim must believe and practice. These precepts are called the Five Pillars of Islam.

The first of these is the recital of the basic profession of Islamic faith: "There is no god but God (Allah) and Muhammad is His prophet." The second precept, or pillar, is that every Muslim must pray five times a day at specific times from before dawn to after sunset. The third precept is that Muslims must give alms or charity to the poor. Some payment of alms is required and some is voluntary. The fourth pillar is that all Muslims are required to fast each year from dawn to dusk throughout the holy month of Ramadan, the month during which Muhammad received the first passages of the Koran. Finally, all Muslims are required to make a pilgrimage to Mecca at least once in a lifetime, assuming they are financially able to.

The Koran

The Koran, or Qur'an, meaning "recitation," is regarded by Muslims as the exact word of God, which was directly revealed to His Prophet Muhammad in the Arabic language. Just as every religion has its prophets, Muhammad regarded himself as the prophet of the Muslims. He was the prophet who would lead the Arabs out of paganism, or the worship of many gods, and bring them to knowledge of the one true God.

According to Muslim beliefs, the Koran completes the earlier revelations recorded in the Bible. Muhammad is the "seal," or last, of the prophets. The messages Muhammad received from God were not written down by the Prophet but by several of his followers. All these passages were collected and placed in some kind of order. Various versions of the Koran were in circulation until 'Uthman, the third caliph (successor to Muhammad), commanded that the version compiled by the scholar Zayd became the one official Koran. All other versions were then destroyed.

The Koran is divided into chapters called suras. In addition to containing the theological, ethical, and juridical teachings of Islam, the Koran is also regarded as a perfect example of the Arabic language and style of writing. For Muslims, the Koran is the earthly copy of the Eternal Book, which is in heaven with God. Because the Koran was revealed to Muhammad in Arabic, this language became the sacred language among the believers in the new religion.

The illustrations below show some fundamental Muslim beliefs and practices.
1. One of the faithful reading the Koran
2. The name of Allah repeated in an interweaving pattern of calligraphic variation. The venerated names of God are frequently the subject of Arabic calligraphers.
3. Prostration takes place several times as part of the ritual act of daily prayer.
4. An illustration of the Archangel Gabriel taken from an Iranian manuscript. Gabriel served sometimes as God's messenger to Muhammad.
5. An illustration of the Ka'aba, the focus of the annual pilgrimage, or hajj, taken from a Turkish manuscript
6. A diagram showing the Prophet's house in Medina. The house was later made into a mosque and is the site of the Prophet's grave.

A mass of pilgrims crowds into the Valley of Mecca during the time of the annual pilgrimage.

THE EARLY ISLAMIC CONQUESTS AND THE FORMATION OF THE MUSLIM EMPIRE

The fierce rivalries that had often characterized relations between Arab tribes asserted itself once more after Muhammad's death. Without the charismatic presence of the Prophet, the unity provided by a common faith soon seemed to be on the verge of collapse.

Muhammad's most faithful followers felt that it was vital to elect a respected man to be the representative or successor of the Prophet. This leader, called the caliph (meaning "deputy"), would continue the work of expanding and consolidating the new faith. Muhammad had not named his successor, but 'Umar (Omar), one of the Prophet's closest friends and most faithful companions, urged the Islamic community to select Abu Bakr as the first caliph. Abu Bakr was the father of A'isha, Muhammad's youngest wife, whom he had wed shortly after Khadija's death. Under Abu Bakr's two-year rule, Islam came to dominate the entire Arabian Peninsula again and began to expand into Syria and into lands now part of Iraq.

Abu Bakr nominated 'Umar to be his successor as the Prophet's deputy. During 'Umar's caliphate, Islam spread throughout the Middle East and North Africa. Islamic armies moved into Syria, Anatolia, Persia, and Egypt. The Muslim armies, inspired by their new religion, had great drive. They easily defeated the more disciplined but slower moving forces of the Byzantine and Persian empires with sudden, swift raids.

Many people living in the conquered lands had been oppressed for centuries by greedy government administrators. This was especially true in rural areas. The Byzantine Empire was also torn by complex struggles between Christian groups. These oppressed people often welcomed the Muslim armies almost as liberators, making it even easier for the Muslims to conquer vast territories.

It was under 'Umar that the administrative and bureaucratic apparatus of Islamic rule began to develop. The Muslims sought to maintain good relations with the subject peoples. A land tax was imposed on all landholders, but a special tax, called the *jizya,* was placed on non-Muslims. The latter tax eventually helped convince many non-Muslims to convert to Islam. Islam was also simpler than the older religions and offered believers an appealing community of belief in which to participate. Of course, many people converted to Islam simply because they found special meaning in the message of Muhammad.

The caliph also directed the organization of the army and the judiciary. He laid down the rules relating to the annual pilgrimage to Mecca. 'Umar instituted a new calendar based on the year of the Hijra and established many other institutions that formed the basis of Muslim society.

After ten years of austere and successful rule, 'Umar was murdered by an angry slave in 644. Before his death, 'Umar delegated a council of six Muslim leaders to select the next caliph. This council chose 'Uthman.

Dissatisfaction grew with 'Uthman's management of finances and the economy. Political intrigues began to threaten the caliph, and he was assassinated in 656. After his death, Ali, Muhammad's first cousin, became the new caliph. Ali was also the Prophet's son-in-law, having married Fatima, Muhammad's daughter.

Ali quickly deposed people in authority in Mecca who opposed him, including A'isha (Muhammad's favorite wife), who had long held a grudge against Ali. But Ali was not able to gain control over Mu'awiyya, the governor of Syria.

Mu'awiyya was the head the of powerful Umayyad clan of Quraysh, and he was closely

The splendid Umayyad mosque in Damascus was built between 705 and 713 by reconstructing the Great Basilica the Roman emperor Theodosius had originally dedicated to St. John the Baptist in 379. The basilica itself had been built on the remains of the pre-Christian Temple of Jupiter, which had been constructed in the 3rd century B.C. on the site of a still earlier place of worship dedicated to the Syrian god Hadad.

related to 'Uthman. Mu'awiyya demanded revenge for 'Uthman's death. Ali refused to provide the satisfaction Mu'awiyya sought. Ali moved against Mu'awiyya militarily. Ultimately, however, Ali was forced to accept a truce with Mu'awiyya in response to demands for preserving the unity of the Muslim *umma*. Ali was assassinated in 661 by a follower of the Kharijite group, a rebel group of Ali's own followers who rejected his agreement to a truce with Mu'awiyya. With Ali's death, Mu'awiyya no longer had any obstacle between himself and the caliphate.

Times had changed, and the new caliph moved his capital from Medina to be closer to his army. Mu'awiyya made Damascus the political and economic capital of the empire, leaving the Arabian cities with their unalterable religious functions.

To the upper right is the gateway to the Qasr al-Khayr al-Sharqi in Syria. This building was an agricultural center, hunting lodge, residence, and post for observing passing caravans. The Umayyad caliphs would spend long periods of time here to escape the intrigues in the capital at Damascus.

To the right are a stucco representation of a dancer and a detail of a wall decoration taken from the Qasr al-Khayr al Gharbi in Syria, a complex of Umayyad buildings and monuments dating from the middle of the 8th century. The complex held a palace, a resting place for caravans, a mosque, and a *hammam*. The *hammam* was much like the public baths of ancient Rome and one of the essential institutions of Islamic city life.

Qusar Amra, Jordan. The "Red Castle" was built by the Umayyad caliph al-Walid I (705-715) as his vacation hunting lodge.

This bronze ewer, or water jug, was made around A.D. 750.

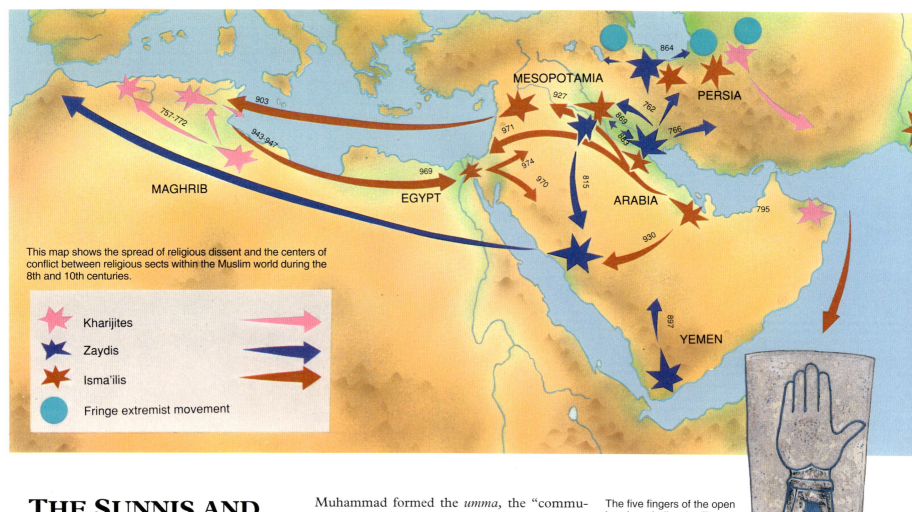

This map shows the spread of religious dissent and the centers of conflict between religious sects within the Muslim world during the 8th and 10th centuries.

★ Kharijites
★ Zaydis
★ Isma'ilis
● Fringe extremist movement

THE SUNNIS AND THE SHI'ITES

A Muslim reading the Koran. The great love Muslims have for their holy book has led many of the faithful to learn whole passages by heart.

Muhammad formed the *umma*, the "community of the faithful," to embrace all people who adhered to the new religion. Some old tribal traditions were rejected altogether, while others were reinterpreted in accordance with the new vision of Islam. The basics of the *umma* included faith and the observance of religious obligations. Islam was closely integrated into the daily life of the faithful and into their social, political, and economic relations.

Muhammad, as God's Prophet, recited several proclamations that moderated many of the aspects of tribal paganism. Some of these guidelines seemed solely dietary in nature, such as forbidding Muslims to eat pork or drink alcoholic beverages. Other injunctions forbid blood feuds and the murder of unwanted female children. In effect, these rules helped change not only people's eating habits but also their overall behavior.

In the eyes of Muslims, the teachings of the Koran, together with the life and example of the Prophet, contain all the necessary principles to guide a person through life and eternal salvation. To this day, this is what the great majority of Muslims, called Sunnis, believe.

The Sunnis form the largest part of the Muslim community and derive their name from the *sunna*, or "path," the traditional practice of Muhammad as recorded in the great collections of Hadith (Traditions).

However, the Sunni interpretation is not recognized by all Muslims in the Islamic world. The unity of belief was broken quite early in Islam's history. Some beliefs of other Muslims are quite close to those of the Sunnis, and some are quite different and distinct.

The five fingers of the open hand symbolize the Five Pillars of Islam. This engraving of an open hand was carved into the keystone of an arched gateway in the Alhambra, in Grenada, Spain.

Above right: An example of the calligraphic decoration giving the name of God with His attributes "Mercy" and "Compassion"

Below right: The clothes and objects show that this Muslim is a Shi'ite.

The first problems arose early over the selection of Muhammad's successor. Since the caliph combined political as well as religious authority, every dissenting faction seemed to merge political aims and motives with religious disagreement.

The first break within the *umma* (or community of Muslims) came from the followers of Ali. These Muslims held that some trace of divine inspiration survived in Muhammad's descendants, and that Muhammad had actually designated Ali as his successor. Therefore this group of Muslims believed that the direct heirs of Ali and Fatima alone had the exclusive right to lead the Islamic *umma*. These dissenters were called Shi'ites, or Shi'a, the party or followers of Ali. Their split with the Sunnis became permanent after Ali's son al-Hussayn and some of his followers were murdered by the Umayyad caliph Yazid in the Iraqi town of Karbala in 680. The date of this murder became one of the most

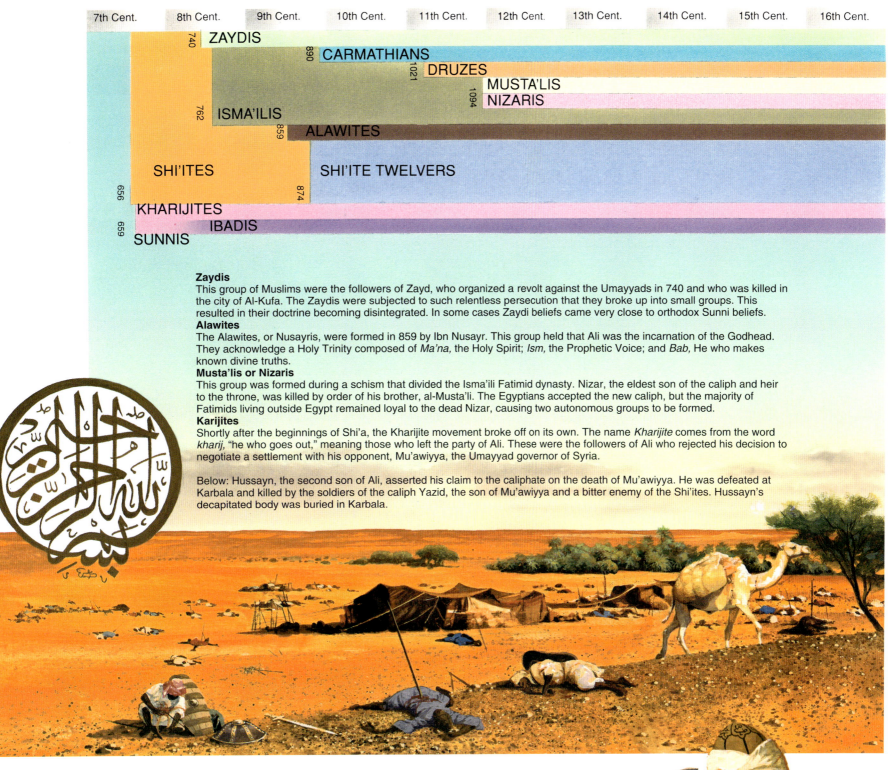

Zaydis
This group of Muslims were the followers of Zayd, who organized a revolt against the Umayyads in 740 and who was killed in the city of Al-Kufa. The Zaydis were subjected to such relentless persecution that they broke up into small groups. This resulted in their doctrine becoming disintegrated. In some cases Zaydi beliefs came very close to orthodox Sunni beliefs.

Alawites
The Alawites, or Nusayris, were formed in 859 by Ibn Nusayr. This group held that Ali was the incarnation of the Godhead. They acknowledge a Holy Trinity composed of *Ma'na*, the Holy Spirit; *Ism*, the Prophetic Voice; and *Bab*, He who makes known divine truths.

Musta'lis or Nizaris
This group was formed during a schism that divided the Isma'ili Fatimid dynasty. Nizar, the eldest son of the caliph and heir to the throne, was killed by order of his brother, al-Musta'li. The Egyptians accepted the new caliph, but the majority of Fatimids living outside Egypt remained loyal to the dead Nizar, causing two autonomous groups to be formed.

Karijites
Shortly after the beginnings of Shi'a, the Kharijite movement broke off on its own. The name *Kharijite* comes from the word *kharij*, "he who goes out," meaning those who left the party of Ali. These were the followers of Ali who rejected his decision to negotiate a settlement with his opponent, Mu'awiyya, the Umayyad governor of Syria.

Below: Hussayn, the second son of Ali, asserted his claim to the caliphate on the death of Mu'awiyya. He was defeated at Karbala and killed by the soldiers of the caliph Yazid, the son of Mu'awiyya and a bitter enemy of the Shi'ites. Hussayn's decapitated body was buried in Karbala.

important days of mourning in the Shi'ite calendar.

The Shi'ites and the Sunnis differ in many respects, but it would be wrong to think that the Shi'ites reject tradition or that the Sunnis do not respect the memory of Ali. In fact, the Shi'ites regard themselves as being more faithful to the concept of tradition than other Muslims are. The Sunnis, for their part, honor Ali as Muhammad's relation, the first male to accept Islam, and the fourth "rightly guided" caliph.

The fundamental difference between the two groups is disagreement over the role of the caliph. The Shi'ites prefer to use the word *imam*, a word which, in itself, is also applied by all Muslims to anyone who leads prayer. But the term *imam* is also used by the Shi'ites to mean the descendant of Ali, who alone should lead the community of the faithful.

The Shi'ite imam, unlike the Sunni caliph, is infallible. He is preserved from sin, and he has superhuman wisdom.

The Shi'ites have a kind of hierarchical clergy unique in Islam. This may be due, in part, to the fact that their creed gradually became the official religion of Persia. The ancient Persian religion of Zoroastrianism also had a powerful and hierarchical priesthood, which may have ultimately influenced Shi'ite Islam.

Over the years, the doctrine concerning the imamate caused the Shi'ites themselves to split into many different sects. The majority sect is called the Twelvers because they accept as legitimate imams twelve of Ali's descendants. The last descendant disappeared mysteriously while still a child. His return is still awaited today.

THE UMAYYAD EMPIRE

Having secured the caliphate, Mu'awiyya's rule was firmly established only in Syria and Egypt. The Kharijites, the Shi'ites, and the many fervent Sunni Muslims in Arabia resented the transfer of the capital from Medina to Damascus. They also disliked the fact that the caliphate had been taken by force.

Even before he assumed the role of caliph, Mu'awiyya had prepared a fleet that enabled him to drive the forces of Byzantium from the Syrian coast. He used the fleet to attack Cyprus, Crete, and Rhodes. In 673 his armies in the east advanced beyond the Oxus River, the river today known as Amu Darya, and military expeditions were sent against the Turks in Bukhara and Samarkand. In the west his forces reached Tripoli in Libya. Constantinople was besieged several times, chiefly after 673.

With regard to internal policies, Mu'awiyya showed himself to be an able ruler. Toward the Syrian-based forces he showed great magnanimity, recognizing that he needed their support to retain power. Damascus became the seat of the splendid Umayyad court, refined and formal in the tradition of the old Mesopotamian kingdoms. The provinces were entrusted to governors chosen from representatives of the most noble Arab families. These governors were allowed considerable autonomy.

Mu'awiyya's successors had to cope with many internal problems. Islam succeeded in penetrating the western part of North Africa, which the Muslims called the Maghrib. But in the east the Byzantines were able to recover some of their lost ground and regain Armenia.

The Umayyad caliph Abd al-Malik and his governor in Iraq, al-Hajjaj, were obliged to make changes to the system of government in order to break old tribal customs. Some of these old customs were making it difficult to obtain unity and obedience in the provinces. The caliph and his governor changed the monetary system, and tribute was again payable by the newly converted. Since there were so many newly converted Muslims, this tax was a good source of revenue.

The Umayyad Age was characterized by the growth of cities, and it gave rise to a highly sophisticated urban culture. Despite the increasingly urban nature of Umayyad society, the motifs of nomadic desert life still dominated Arab poetry. Although genuine nomads never accounted for more than a small minority of the population of the Arabian Peninsula, their military dominance in the life of pre-Islamic Arabia continued to exercise a lasting impact on Arab literature. A respect, love, and longing for the values of nomadic life also served to safeguard the traditions of a ruling class that, while still Arab, was now increasingly infused with many foreign peoples.

Four other cities apart from Damascus developed rapidly in the Umayyad period. The cities were al-Fustat in Egypt and Basra, Al-Kufa, and Wasit in Iraq. They had started as garrison towns for Arab troops stationed in the provinces, but little by little they became centers for civilian populations.

The Umayyad Empire reached the height of its power between 709 and 713. Muslim armies conquered Transoxiana (the fertile lands to the east of the Oxus River in western Asia) and the cities of Bukhara, Samarkand, and Kabul in Central Asia. With the conquest of Multan, they reached the Indus River, and the north Indian plateau lay before them.

In 711, the same year that the Muslims were conquering Samarkand, the Muslim general Tariq ibn Ziad led an army into the Iberian Peninsula. Only two years later Islamic armies crossed the Pyrenees Mountains between Spain and France and reached the Frankish town of Narbonne in what is now southern France.

The Arabs continued to advance into the land of the Franks as far as Poitiers (south of Paris), where in 732 they were stopped by Charles Martel. The Muslim retreat from southern France began only after 759, when Pépin III reconquered Narbonne.

The caliph al-Walid also wanted to give splendor to his reign. Workers and artists, especially Byzantines, were summoned to extend or build new mosques and palaces that would be monuments to his dynasty. Meanwhile, the Arabs consolidated control of the empire, promoted by reforms such as the prohibition of Christians from holding administrative office.

In 717 'Umar II became caliph. He encouraged conversion to Islam among non-Arabs, reduced taxes, and tried to promote a fair system of taxation by imposing a land tax on all men, including Muslims. He also tried to make peace with the Shi'ites.

After the brief reign of 'Umar II, the empire began to tear itself apart. Some Arab tribes demanded a superior position in the empire. Meanwhile, non-Arab converts to Islam resented such second-class status.

The geographical extent of the Muslim conquests together with poor communications also isolated Damascus from the farthest reaches of the empire. It became impossible to maintain order in the provinces, and the inadequacy of the last Umayyad caliphs promoted anarchy.

One of the most powerful Arab clans in Mecca, the Abbasids, had been quietly supporting and financing uprisings, especially among non-Arab Muslims known as Mawaali. Their chief, Abu al-'Abbas, finally decided that the time was right for open revolt. With great speed the Abbasid Revolution overcame the Umayyads, who were slaughtered except for a young Umayyad prince named Abd al-Rahman, who fled to Spain and founded the Umayyad dynasty of Córdoba.

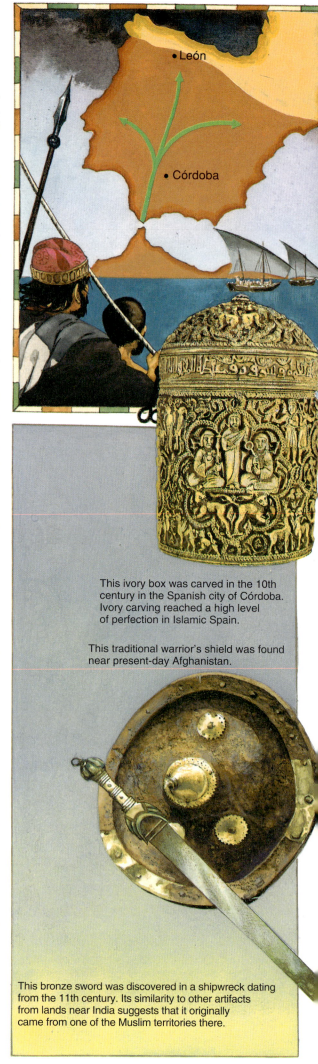

This ivory box was carved in the 10th century in the Spanish city of Córdoba. Ivory carving reached a high level of perfection in Islamic Spain.

This traditional warrior's shield was found near present-day Afghanistan.

This bronze sword was discovered in a shipwreck dating from the 11th century. Its similarity to other artifacts from lands near India suggests that it originally came from one of the Muslim territories there.

Tariq ibn Ziad was a freed Berber slave who became governor of Tangier. He brought Islam to Spain when he invaded the Iberian Peninsula in 711.

The black kite is a bird of prey native to Bactria, an ancient region that is today part of Afghanistan. This bird is frequently depicted on royal seals and amulets discovered in archaeological excavations of the ancient settlements of this region. Falconry is a popular sport in the eastern Arab world.

A typical nomad encampment in Bactria. Muslim conquerors passed through this area before crossing the Oxus River. From the time of the Bronze Age, there had been rich and refined civilizations here.

ABBASID INSTITUTIONS, ECONOMY, AND SOCIAL STRUCTURE

The Abbasid caliphs moved the capital eastward from Damascus to their new capital, Baghdad. Their name is associated with the most splendid period of medieval Islamic culture and civilization.

This was a time of profound change in Islamic society, especially in Islam's political and administrative institutions. The elevation of the caliph by dynastic succession was no longer questioned.

The refined and autocratic Abbasid court was the heart of the empire. Its pomp and magnificence resembled that of the earlier Sassanian dynasty in Persia. Privileged positions at court were granted only to those whom the caliph favored, and his choice was no longer governed exclusively by considerations of Arab tribal heritage. This change diminished the influence of the great Arab tribal clans in favor of the caliph's "family" and retainers.

The harem, coming from the Arabic word for "forbidden," was that private part of the palace reserved for wives, young children, eunuchs, and concubines. The harem became the scene of important political decisions. It was also often the center for palace intrigues, which often troubled the Abbasid dynasty.

The social structure of the Abbasid world was like a pyramid. At its base, one step above slaves, were the mass of subjects with few political rights. At the top of the social pyramid was the caliph with his absolute power. The only guarantee of protection of individual rights lay in the law of Islam, to which even the caliph supposedly had to submit. Upholding religion was his primary responsibility.

In his political function as head of state the caliph was assisted by a vizier, whose function can be compared to that of a prime minister. Under him were ranks of secretaries, tax collectors, and military leaders.

Ultimately, administration in the Abbasid state was subject to the will of the caliph or a particularly influential vizier. However, the Abbasids did create *diwans,* or ministries, to manage a wide range of affairs.

One highly important *diwan* dealt with official communications and secret information. This

1. This bronze perfume burner is shaped like a bird of prey. It was made in Persia in the late 8th century or early 9th century.

2. This terra-cotta plate shows an Islamic knight in full armor astride a splendidly outfitted horse. The plate was probably made in Persia near the end of the 9th century.

3. Ukhaidir. This fortified palace in Mesopotamia was built in the 8th century. It has the typical floor plan of a Sassanian palace complex. Unlike the majority of Mesopotamian palaces, which are built of bricks, this palace was constructed of stone chips bound with mortar.

4. An armed guard of the caliph's court

5. The caliph and his dignitaries proceed with pomp and ceremony across the Court of Honor in the Palace of Ukhaidir.

The Round City of al-Mansur

In 762 al-Mansur decided to demonstrate Abbasid glory by building a completely new capital for his government. Thus began the construction of the famed round city on the west bank of the Tigris River. It took four years to build the magnificent city, called Baghdad, splendid heir of the ancient capital of Babylon.

The city of al-Mansur, also called Madinat as-Salam, the "city of peace," was surrounded by a ditch 65 feet wide. The city's embankments and walls divided it into corresponding concentric areas that could be sealed off from one another by a system of gates. In the center stood the caliph's palace, the most important *diwans*, and the great mosque.

At first the commercial district was far from the city's center, and it was divided into four symmetrical areas delineated by the four main entrance gates to the city. But the commercial district was very soon transferred outside the city walls.

The residential areas were on the east bank of the Tigris. They formed a huge city in themselves with a wealth of splendid palaces and gardens. The dwellings of the poor could be found in outlying districts.

agency was in charge of postal services, run with a network of carrier pigeons, and espionage.

The *diwan* for the army and the caliph's bodyguard were a source of continual financial drain, especially as the age of Muslim conquest came to a halt. The caliph could no longer rely on a small elite and homogeneous cadre of Arab nobility, as the Umayyad were able to. Therefore, the Abbasids found themselves increasingly relying on foreign mercenaries.

The *diwan* for the maintenance of order ran the police service. In Baghdad alone there were about 10,000 police officers, and the official in charge of them was empowered to act with considerable freedom.

Originally, government officials of the various provinces were given only local responsibilities, since all important matters had to remain under the control of the caliph. With the decline in caliphal power, however, the discontent and ambition of the provincial governors caused many rifts. Rival caliphates in Cairo and Córdoba were ultimately declared by the year 929. In Iraq the caliph had to accept increasing protection from Turkic peoples, who were soon to decide the fate of Islam.

THE ABBASIDS— A BLENDING OF MANY DIFFERENT PEOPLES

The territories conquered by Islam expanded further during the early Abbasid Age, but these conquests remained uncertain, mirroring the tensions that permeated the caliphate. In 849 the caliph al-Mutasim decided that Baghdad had become too dangerous and unstable. He moved the capital to Samarra, about 60 miles northwest of Baghdad, where the court remained for about 50 years. In this period there was an attempt to resolve political and social problems in the empire by implementing an unyielding orthodoxy, which was particularly hard on religious minorities, such as Christians and Jews.

What had formerly been Roman Africa now entered a period of great splendor. The port of Carthage became a base for raids by Muslim pirates. Their raids were directed against Italy, where they laid waste the countryside around Rome and Naples and even made attacks on Genoa and Venice. In France the Muslim forces established a similar bridgehead at La Garde Freinet in Provence, from which they made further raids.

The special feature of the Abbasid dynasty, however, was that it gave rise to a truly multiethnic Muslim Empire in place of the almost exclusively Arab Empire of the Umayyads. The Arab element was by no means ousted by the changes imposed by the new caliphs. The Arabic language was still the official language of the vast empire, and the ruling dynasty itself still boasted of pure Arab ancestry. It took its very name from Abbas, Muhammad's uncle.

Aspects of Arab culture survived in Muslim culture. However, they now gradually blended with the intellectual and artistic heritages of the other peoples and civilizations of the Middle East.

A particularly striking development was that the Arabs were no longer regarded as the sole guardians of either the Islamic faith or the institutions most suited to governing the empire. The various peoples who collectively formed the Islamic community successfully claimed the right to consider themselves an integral part of the new order. The Muslim world was to be governed by retaining the best of the traditions of the different ethnic groups which it incorporated.

New principles of Muslim law were developed. Some of these principles took on the thorny problem of taxation, which had already created huge difficulties for the Umayyad caliphs earlier. The treasury was reorganized on more equitable lines, with taxation being changed from personal to property tax.

The fame of the Abbasid Age is usually associated with three caliphs. Their rule corresponded to three long periods of order and stability.

Al-Mansur, the second Abbasid caliph and true founder of the dynasty, ruled from 754 to 775, a period of some 20 years. During this time, he established government organization along ancient Persian lines with a very powerful caliph.

Harun, known as al-Rashid, the "Well led," was caliph from 786 to 809. His rule is remembered as one of the periods of greatest prosperity. In the West he is renowned chiefly as the caliph of Baghdad in the collection of stories entitled *A Thousand and One Nights*.

Lastly, al-Mamun, caliph from 813 to 833, was a patron of artists and men of culture. He helped make Baghdad an unrivaled center of science and literature. The first astronomical observatory in the Islamic world was built under the patronage of this caliph. In this observatory the

Common people, soldiers, and merchants gathered around the Great Mosque of Samarra to talk and do business. It is perhaps the largest mosque in the world. Built in 847, today only the surrounding walls and the remarkable spiral minaret remain. The minaret is over 160 feet high. The outer walls are reinforced with semicircular buttresses. The mosque had 16 gates.

Right: This ground plan of the Great Mosque of Samarra shows a forest of octagonal pillars occupying much of the court and supporting the roof. The pillars were linked to each other with roof beams. In the center of the plan lies the open courtyard.

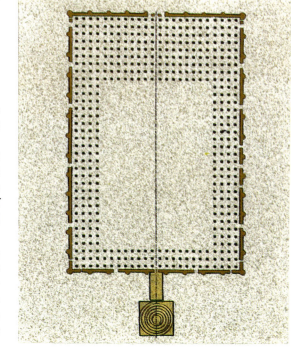

The heart of the Abbasid Empire, showing the cities that played an important role in the history of the caliphate.

The Cities of the Caliphs

The Abbasid Age brought even greater development of cities than the preceding epoch. New cities were founded, some were expanded, and still others were redesigned. Every settlement bore witness to Islam's enormous capacity to absorb preexisting traditions and enrich them.

The caliphs employed architects and local workers, such as artisans and skilled technicians, to build their cities. The Great Mosque of Samarra echoes the shape of the ancient Mesopotamian ziggurats, or temple towers. The city of Fez in present-day Morocco was founded long after the fall of Rome and after numerous barbarian raids had all but destroyed city life in this area. Fez was a city of eastern design in the midst of a rural Berber society. The cities of the Mediterranean retained many of their ancient characteristics, but they also acquired distinctive Islamic features.

Right: This fish-shaped, decorative gold pin was made in Iran during the 7th or 8th century.
Below right: The remains of the Balkuwara Palace built between 854 and 859 for the caliph al-Mutazz.

greatest Muslim scientists studied the positions of the stars, paving the way for the later discoveries of European astronomers, such as Kepler and Copernicus.

Writers and scientists also gained fame through their works. In the 11th century a Muslim scholar of Persian heritage, al-Biruni, helped spread Islam further east through the circulation of his maxims, fables, and scientific writings.

The late Abbasid period saw the revival of the mystical movement in Islam known as Sufism. Among the most famous Sufis were the martyr al-Hallaj, who was put to death in 922 for asserting his union with God, and al-Ghazali, who found a way of linking legal and philosophical thought with mystical experience.

ARTISTIC SPLENDOR AND PHILOSOPHY

The golden age of Islamic art and science does not coincide with the time of the greatest Muslim military and political strength. In fact the great flowering of Muslim culture took place when the caliphate was already troubled by the internal tensions that would lead to its downfall.

In the days of the caliph al-Mamun the cultural supremacy of the Muslim countries was already acknowledged in the West. Arabic was considered the language of scholars.

The Figurative Arts

A distinctive style of Islamic art had already emerged during the Umayyad Age, with the introduction of such architectural features as the horseshoe arch, the minaret, and mosaic decoration derived from Byzantine models. However, during the Abbasid Age, the Islamic artistic heritage was enriched by new architectural designs and decorative features from other civilizations.

New structures appeared. One was the *iwan*, a great arch-shaped hall with a barrel vault. The *iwan* was derived from the Persian public-audience halls of the Sassanian period. Another structure, called *muqarnas*, was also developed at this time. *Muqarnas* was a kind of transitional bridging element used as a cornice between the walls and the ceiling or a cupola.

Ceramic art flourished during the Abbasid Age, but there was a general absence in the Islamic world of the figurative arts, namely painting and sculpture. Some jurists, especially in the Sunni world, interpreted Islamic law as prohibiting the depiction of human or animal forms. These rules may have stemmed from the belief that it was sacrilegious to represent the human face.

On the other hand, architecture and the applied arts flourished in the Muslim world. With the exception of minarets, early Islamic buildings were seldom tall. Nevertheless, because of their open structure and fretwork, they did not appear heavy.

The decoration of walls and ceilings with flowing and brightly colored geometric designs accentuated the grace and appearance of buildings by masking their structural elements. The artistry of such decoration has become a distinctive feature of Islamic art. Amazing results were also achieved in calligraphy, which is the production of words, or entire sentences, combining the most elegant forms of script and design.

Finally, the minor arts should not be forgotten. Bronze objects, painted ceramics, precious metals, carpets, and miniature paintings on paper all reached an exceptionally high level of refinement and perfection in the Islamic world.

Literature

Poetry was the great literary form of pre-Islamic Arabia. Arab and Persian poetry remained very important in the Islamic period. In prose, too, there were remarkable achievements by the Arab people, both in narrative and essay writing.

Islamic scholars wrote essays on many subjects, from the interpretation of the Koran to philosophy, law, history, and the various sciences. They also wrote many commentaries on the Traditions, or Hadith, concerning the Prophet.

Philosophy and the Sciences

Philosophy and the exact sciences in the Muslim world, as in classical Greece and Rome, were closely linked. However, those who devoted themselves only to theoretical speculation were very often regarded by Muslim religious scholars with skepticism and sometimes even suspected of heresy, par-

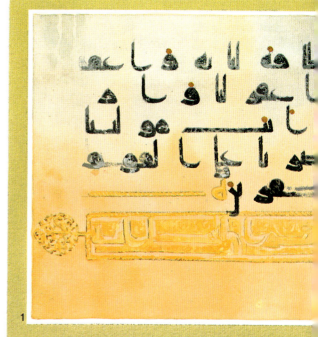

1. A page of the Koran in Kufic script. This script was named after the city of Al-Kufa, an important cultural and scientific center in Iraq where this style first emerged. Kufic script was used in the earliest days of Arab-Islamic writing between the 7th and 10th centuries.

2. A relief, or wall carving, showing a horseman killing a bear. This relief is part of the exterior decoration of the Church of Akhtamar, which was built during the 10th century in Armenia. This church bears eloquent testimony to the meeting of Christian and Islamic art, as illustrated by these scenes of Abbasid court life.

3. Shown below is a 17th-century Persian astrolabe, an instrument used for making astronomical observations and calculations. Believed to have been known to the Greeks, although no examples or precise descriptions survive from antiquity, it was perfected and used by Muslim scientists.

4. The celestial globe to the right was made in 1050 by the Spanish scientist Ibrahim ibn Sa'id and his son Muhammad.

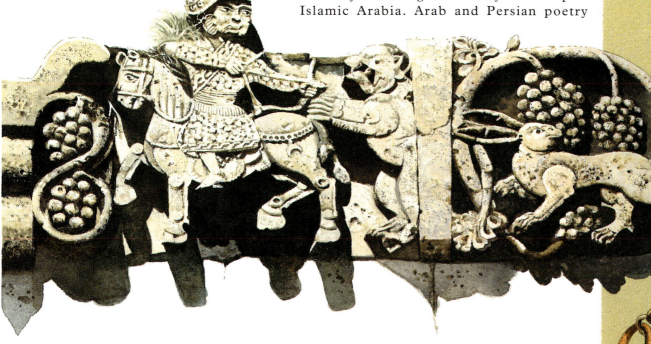

ticularly if they came too close to the rationalism of Western thought. Avicenna, the most famous medieval Muslim philosopher, and a great interpreter of Aristotle, always subordinated the axioms of the Greek philosophers to the truths revealed in the Koran.

Islamic scientists prospered in every field. Agronomists, mineralogists, geographers, astronomers, mathematicians, chemists, and physicians all made great progress in their fields. The West is indebted to the Islamic world for the wealth of knowledge in these disciplines. To al-Khwarizmi (from whose name we derive the mathematical term *algorithm*) and to al-Battani, we owe the spread of algebra, the invention of the sine and the tangent, and studies on elliptic inclination. To the chemist Jabir b. Hayyan, we owe the technique of distillation and the description of elements such as alcohol and sulfuric acid. Last, the great physician al-Razi bequeathed to us his important studies on smallpox and other infectious diseases, thereby enriching our knowledge of pharmacology.

Above: The figures in the scene are *ulama*, or religious scholars of Islam. They are seen studying and discussing theological, philosophical, and juridical matters in a *madrassa*, or "college" of higher religious scholarship.

5. The large ceramic vase above was made in the late 12th century. Black decoration on a light or, as in this case, turquoise background became typical of ceramics from the northern Mesopotamian area.

6. The Syrian incense burner was made of inlaid brass during the second half of the 13th century.

The ornamentation of metalwork, with inlaid designs in gold or silver, is still called damascening after the city of Damascus where it originated.

This Arab ship of the late Middle Ages shows the rudder hinged at the center of the stern. This was an innovation in traditional boats of the time, which employed twin rudders at the sides.

Muslim ships, bearing the name of Allah on their sails, pull away from the coast.

The Arabs developed at least two major advances in navigation technique: the magnetic compass and the lateen sail. The magnetic compass, which was probably first invented by the Chinese, was introduced to Europe by the Arabs. The lateen sail was a triangular or trapezoidal sail, which catches the wind better in the Mediterranean than square sails.

THE ARMY AND THE FLEET

As with most medieval societies, the arts of war were important in the Islamic world. The pre-Islamic Arab tribes regarded any man capable of bearing arms as a potential warrior. The early battles that enabled Islam to spread with such lightning speed initially were not very different from traditional Bedouin raids. Muslim warriors, armed with lances, arrows, and swords and riding on horses and camels, carried out sudden fierce raids that scattered their enemies.

With a rapidly expanding empire and with increased wealth consequently at their disposal, Muslim leaders soon felt the need for a better organized army. The second "rightly-guided" caliph, 'Umar, created a kind of "ministry of war," a council to run the army, which listed the names of warriors according to family and tribe. The council drew up lists of soldiers or tribes to go on expeditions and developed criteria for dividing the booty taken. The last Umayyad caliph, Marwan II, formed a standing army consisting largely of non-Arab soldiers in place of the contingents of Arab tribesmen that dominated the early Islamic conquests.

The Caliphal Army

The strength of the first caliphal army was its light cavalry, which harassed enemy infantry on their flanks, taking advantage of any gaps to break up their ranks. In these situations the cavalryman's favorite weapons were the lance and bow.

The tribe did not disappear entirely as a fighting unit. As the empire grew, however, other elements, including slaves, mercenaries, non-Muslims, and new converts, joined the growing ranks of the huge army.

This differentiation in the composition of troops was reflected strategically in the different tactics adopted. The regular troops would advance slowly, ready for great frontal assaults, whereas armed tribal units would either go ahead to wear down the enemy with short sharp attacks or would follow behind to raid and plunder.

The standing army mirrored the evolution of the empire which, by extending its boundaries, was destined to come increasingly under foreign influences. From the Byzantines, the Muslim

Opposite page: 1. The illustration directly above shows flags brought by the soldiers to the Battle of Siffin in 657. This was the climactic battle between the forces of Ali, the fourth caliph, and Mu'awiyya, the Umayyad governor of Syria.
2. The saber at the top left is said to have belonged to the Prophet Muhammad.
3. Turkish sabers made between the 9th and 13th centuries
4. Turkish saber from the Altai Mountains, 8th century. Weapons, soldiers, and strategies of Turkish origin were already finding their place in the Abbasid army during the 9th century.

Above right: These different types of warriors are representative of the various backgrounds of soldiers in the caliph's army. These soldiers helped to introduce local customs into Islamic culture: 1. Azerbaijan infantryman in the early 10th century; 2. Knight of the Fatimid army in the 11th century; 3. Horseman from Transoxiana in the late 9th century.

army adopted catapults and siege machines; from the Sassanids and the Franks, they borrowed heavy cavalry and fortified structures. To a lesser extent the Berbers, the Kurds, the Armenians, and others also introduced some of their own military traditions into the Islamic army. From the 10th century onward, the borders of Islam were dotted with *ribats,* secluded barrack outposts designed to harbor those who fought both for the physical expansion of the Muslim world and who waged spiritual war against temptation of the soul.

The Islamic art of warfare reached its peak between the 12th and 13th centuries. Armies in this period were led by great commanders, such as Saladin and Baybars I. These armies were known for their discipline and religious fervor. The strategic mobility of Muslim armies in the later Middle Ages was backed by secure bases for supplies and provisions, among which were fortresses seized from the Crusaders. Muslim armies were also renowned for their efficient communications and numerous war machines. They were guaranteed a plentiful supply of weapons from an active and sophisticated arms manufacturing industry.

The Fleet

The fleet, launched in the 7th century by 'Uthman, the third Islamic caliph, was not ultimately able to keep up with the expanding empire. As a desert people, the Arabs had few naval traditions of their own. So, faced with the Mediterranean and the obvious advantages a capable fleet would offer in the way of conquests and booty, the Arabs quickly learned Roman and Byzantine techniques of naval warfare. For example, they adopted the traditional Roman galley with many oars and anchors fore and aft. Although navigation techniques in the Mediterranean during the early Middle Ages were the same for Muslims and Christians, the naval tactics developed by Muslim fleets soon made them masters of the Mediterranean Sea.

Islamic strategy emphasized avoiding naval battles at all costs. Instead they relied on piracy and highly effective raids. One such raid in 846 defeated an enemy fleet of 73 ships, with 11,000 men and 500 horses, in an estuary of the Tiber River.

IRAN AND ISLAM

Modern-day Iran was once called Persia. It was the cradle of a great and ancient Indo-European civilization long before the rise of Islam.

The land of Iran is part of a huge plateau surrounded by mountain chains with some peaks higher than 20,000 feet. The plateau has many deep basins that contain lakes or salt marshes. Iran has cold winters and warm summers with great temperature variations. Winds that blow from the northern regions increase the aridity of the land. Little can grow in such arid land except in low-lying areas near the water table and along some coastal areas on the Persian Gulf and Caspian Sea.

Islam penetrated the ancient lands of Persia very early. In 641 'Umar's cavalry forced its way across the plateau and occupied the major cities of Persia. The Islamic armies encountered much more difficulty than they experienced in other regions because of the high mountain chains which encircle the Plateau of Iran.

Persia played a key role in the formation of Islamic civilization, enriching it with its own ancient culture and traditions. From Darius, Cyrus, and Xerxes to the Sassanian dynasty, the Persians had always played a central role in the history of the Middle East. Persia inspired Abbasid court pomp and ceremony, as well as some of the methods of government. The Persian language, despite the adoption of the Arabic alphabet, continued to survive in Iran as the primary language and as an important means of literary expression. The distinctive geographical and cultural features of this region constantly made it the center of political and artistic development.

The first important dynasty to occupy vast areas of Iran was the Saffarid dynasty, founded by Ya'qub ibn Layth al-Saffar. Initially, al-Saffar had the caliph's approval because he had helped to put an end to the bloodthirsty attacks of the fanatical Kharajites in the remote province of Sistan.

In the summer of 875, however, Ya'qub found himself in conflict with the caliph, who did not want to accept Saffarid dominion in Fars, a region close to Iraq. Ya'qub's army defeated the caliph's forces, and when Ya'qub died, his brother inherited the important provinces of Fars, Khorasan, Kurdistan, and Sistan. Saffarid power soon came to an end when, in 902, the caliph al-Mu'tadid ordered the Saffarid's territory attacked by the Samanids, who gradually occupied it.

Iran and the Surrounding Regions

The funeral rites and edifices of orthodox Islam were theoretically very simple. Throughout the Muslim Empire, however, we find examples of magnificent monumental tombs, such as this mausoleum built by the Samanids of Bukhara in the 10th century.

A silver vase made sometime between the 8th and 10th centuries

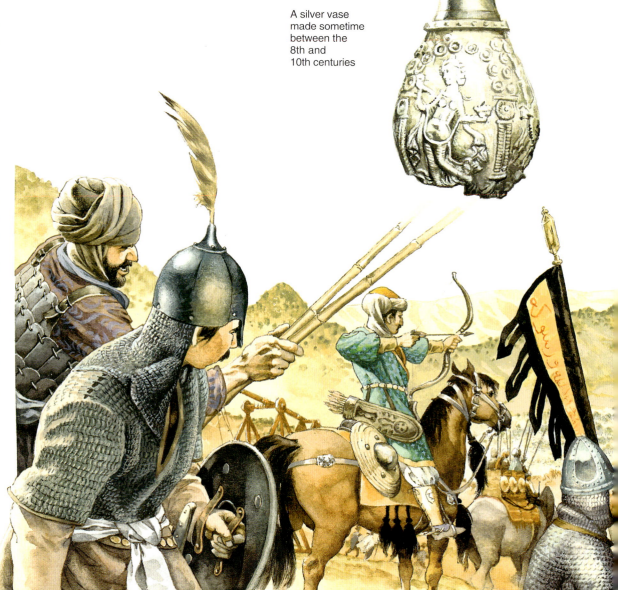

Mahamud of Ghazna, the great Ghaznavid commander whose power reached as far as India, attacks an enemy fortress using catapults and elephant charges. This episode occurred in 1003 in the Sistan region.

A bronze oil lamp (10th and 11th centuries)

The founder of this new dynasty was a Persian who originally believed in the ancient Persian religion Zoroastrianism. He converted to Islam, and he and his family were distinguished by their loyalty to the Abbasid caliphs.

The heartland of Samanid power was Transoxiana, whose principal cities, Bukhara and Samarkand, became important centers of culture, attracting artists, scientists, and intellectuals such as the philosopher Avicenna. The geographer Haukal wrote about the magnificence of Transoxiana's buildings and gardens.

In fact the Samanids ruled over most of Persia and even beyond, as far as the borders of India. There were nine Samanid rulers, but the power of the family began to wane because of internal conflicts that tore it apart after the death of the third ruler in 942. One of the vast number of Turkish slaves who served at the Samanid court, Sebüktigin, took advantage of the situation. In 999 he started the Ghaznavid dynasty, occupying the territories to the south of the Oxus River.

After 950, the Abbasid caliphs fell under the control of a powerful Shi'ite clan known as the Buyids. Although the Abbasid caliph continued to rule the empire in name, the Buyid viziers held real political and military power for over a century.

One of the Buyids, Ahmad, known as Mu'izz al-Dawla, or "fortifier of the state," deposed the caliph al-Mustakfi in 946 and chose as his successor the more malleable al-Muti. Al-Muti's grandson, in turn, succeeded in reuniting Persia and Iraq and keeping the peace for some 30 years. He was known not only for his love of literature and the arts but also for his philanthropy and religious piety. Al-Muti's grandson founded a hospital in Baghdad and had a great mausoleum built in honor of Ali on the spot where it was thought Ali was buried. At the death of al-Muti's grandson, the inevitable struggles over the succession brought an end to the Buyid dynasty, the final blow being the occupation of Baghdad by the Seljuk Turk Toghril Beg in 1055.

Above left: A rice field in the Mazandaran region of Persia, bordered by the Caspian Sea in the north and the Elborz Mountains in the south. There are many valleys in this area, which is crossed by rivers flowing down to the sea to form a fertile alluvial plain. The coast of the Caspian Sea with its rich vegetation contrasts sharply with the dry conditions of the Iranian interior.

Left: The pomegranate is native to Iran, where it is cultivated and also grows wild.

An orange tree. The name of the ancient city of Jiroft in the southeastern part of Iran means "paradise." The name may have derived from the splendid gardens of citrus fruits that once existed in the city. Jiroft was abandoned after the ruinous Mongol invasions of the 13th and 14th centuries.

TRADE AND TRADE ROUTES

Under Islamic control, the Middle East continued to serve as a bridge between Europe and Asia. As in antiquity, the Middle East was the center of a huge network of trade and communications networks linked by land and sea. Muslim merchants carried Islam with them far beyond the forward positions of Muslim armies. Trade, therefore, served as an important vehicle for encouraging conversion to Islam.

Maritime trade in the Indian Ocean and the Mediterranean and Red seas saw increasing traffic thanks to the resurgence of Egypt under the Fatimids. These waters were filled with vessels loaded with merchandise destined for the ports of both the East and the West. The strategic locations of cities such as Baghdad and Samarra also attracted merchants' interests towards the Persian Gulf. Some Muslim merchant ships sailed as far as Korea and Malaysia, and Muslim merchants established trading colonies on the coasts of India.

Shipping was sometimes a dangerous way to conduct trade, given the quality of ships and the presence of pirates, yet the sea provided a much cheaper avenue of transport than overland transit. However, some important new overland routes were generally opened. These routes were developed for the transportation of goods by camel caravans.

These overland trade routes became the realm of great caravans traveling in every direction. Long lines of camels, and other beasts of burden, sometimes numbered more than 5,000 animals. These caravans were laden with merchandise, and they stopped along their routes and conducted business at rest institutions, called caravansaries, situated along the great trade routes.

Also called khans, caravansaries were usually large enclosed buildings, which included a hotel, storerooms, and even small mosques. Often caravansaries were fortified to protect caravans from raids. There were also many smaller resting places at oases and wells where caravans might pause to rest.

After leaving the heart of the Muslim world, the travel routes stretched beyond Persia to India and China. From these regions came slaves, furs, and weapons from Turkestan; paper, silk, and porcelain from China; musk from Tibet; and precious cloth from Kashmir. Islamic money, the silver dirham and the gold dinar, was of high quality and valued everywhere.

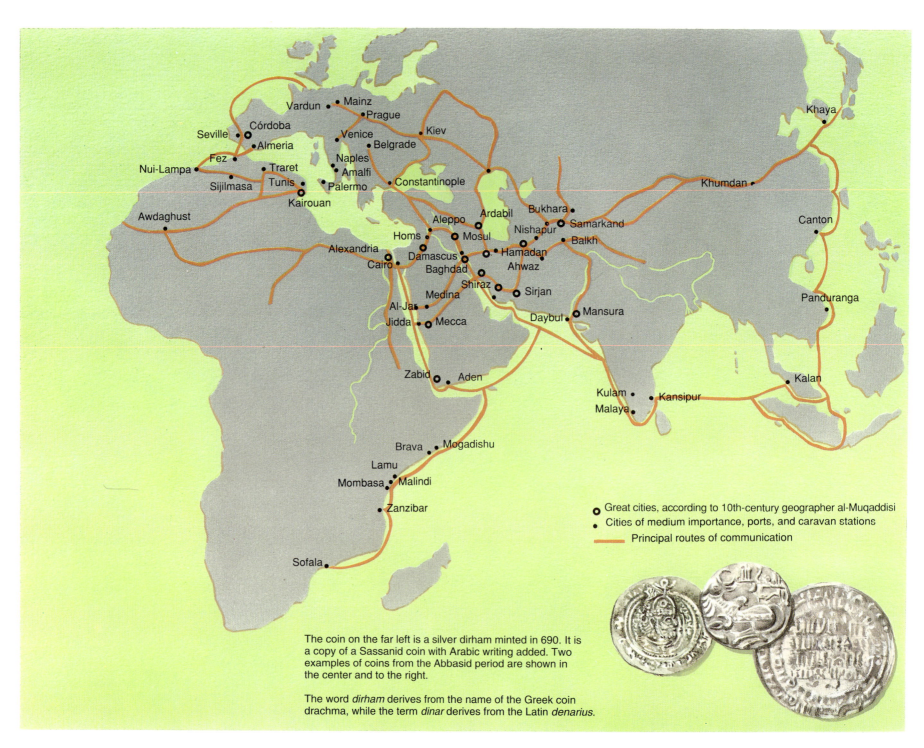

○ Great cities, according to 10th-century geographer al-Muqaddisi
• Cities of medium importance, ports, and caravan stations
— Principal routes of communication

The coin on the far left is a silver dirham minted in 690. It is a copy of a Sassanid coin with Arabic writing added. Two examples of coins from the Abbasid period are shown in the center and to the right.

The word *dirham* derives from the name of the Greek coin *drachma*, while the term *dinar* derives from the Latin *denarius*.

From Southeast Asia, Muslim traders procured luxury goods, such as perfumes, spices, pearls, ivory, precious stones, and Malay tin, in exchange for manufactured articles. From both West and East Africa, Muslim traders obtained gold and great numbers of slaves.

The European region also provided slaves, as well as precious cloths and other sought-after goods. Timber, honey, and furs came from the Russian forests, and from Byzantium and Western Europe came brocades and other prized articles.

Merchants grouped together into loose trading partnerships and societies. They built warehouses and inns, called *funduq*, to facilitate business in the most important cities along the trade routes.

There were still taxes, tolls, customs duties, delayed payment systems, and bills of exchange. Lending money was complicated since the payment of interest was technically prohibited by Islamic law.

By the second half of the 10th century, Arabian geographers were already marking on their maps the seaports of Naples, Gaeta, Amalfi, and Venice, all centers of the mercantile renaissance in the Christian West. The great economic vitality of the Muslim world undoubtedly contributed to the revival of Europe in the 11th century. In the Mediterranean basin, constant trade encouraged the use of Arabic as a common language for centuries.

The great long-distance merchants, as opposed to simple shopkeepers, formed a privileged social class. They were sometimes extremely wealthy and frequently made loans, both voluntarily and forced, to the government. To simplify their accounting, they adopted the Indian numeral system.

Top left: This illustration shows the reconstruction of a large caravansary that once existed in what is now Turkmenistan in Central Asia. The lower illustration shows a detail of a caravansary with a raised mosque in Asia Minor.

Below: Crowds throng the *suq,* or market, one of the most characteristic features of Islamic cities. Stores line the narrow streets and alleys. Some of the stores that sell food have open fronts. Other stores are closed. The narrow streets and alleys form the *suq,* which is almost a city within the city. This busy area is typical of every Islamic city center, with streets or whole areas assigned to the production and sale of particular goods.

Farmlands at the mouth of the Tigris River

AGRICULTURAL PRODUCTION AND FARMING TECHNIQUES

When Islam spread out from the desert lands of the Arabian Peninsula, it encountered lands with very ancient agricultural traditions. The lands of the Fertile Crescent, Mesopotamia and Egypt, were blessed by the waters of the Tigris-Euphrates and Nile rivers. The lands of the Maghrib had once supplied the Roman Empire with agricultural produce as well.

These regions continued to raise their traditional crops under Muslim rule. They even sought to improve the quality and quantity of crops. Some crops were also raised in new areas of the empire. Pulse crops from the Maghrib were successfully raised in Spain. New kinds of fruits and vegetables appeared in markets in the West. These were cultivated first in Spain and Sicily and in time were grown successfully in other parts of Europe. Among these fruits and vegetables were apricots and plums from Syria and Palestine; and melons, cauliflower, and artichokes from other parts of the Islamic world.

The Islamic world acquired sugarcane and rice from the East. Both were eventually grown in the damp, low-lying areas of Jordan, the south of Morocco, Upper Egypt, and even in Spain. Lastly, from Africa, south of the Sahara, came sorghum and dates.

Land was still cultivated with traditional Mediterranean farming methods, employing three basic tools: the mattock, the plow, and the waterwheel. Ancient Persian or Mesopotamian systems of irrigation were also improved. Results were so impressive that the new methods were soon adopted in the Western world.

Irrigation techniques used by the ancient South Arabians were now used in many Islamic lands. Among these techniques was the use of runnels, or small streams and brooks that take advantage of the natural differences in the level of the land to transport water from place to place. A more complicated method of irrigation was the use of a noria, or waterwheel, to raise water from canals and dump it into irrigation trenches.

Raising livestock was a traditional activity of the Arabs. This industry, too, benefited from the introduction of more scientific methods of selective breeding. New and highly prized breeds of sheep and horses were sold in the marketplace. Thoroughbred Arabian stallions were in great demand throughout Europe.

The Peasants

Although agriculture in the Muslim world flourished, the peasant class still held a low place in the social order. Farm laborers and small landholders were oppressed by the large landowners and harassed by marauding brigands and soldiers. Merchants charged the peasants high prices for goods, and nomad tribes trampled across the land with their livestock. However, it was the pressure of often oppressive taxation that ruined many peasants and drove them into the cities.

The Artisan

The raw materials brought by merchants to the cities enabled artisans to produce articles on a large scale, and their excellent work was in high demand everywhere in the medieval world. Artisans organized themselves into guilds. Whole streets and quarters of a city were reserved for particular trades. The business district of Tunis had its famous *suq* of the perfume makers, and the city of al-Mansur, Baghdad itself, was planned to provide districts specially designed for various crafts.

The actual techniques employed by the artisans developed and changed in response to the demand for new articles to replace traditional ones. For example, in textiles, cotton almost completely replaced linen as a favorite fabric. Silk was not only imported from China but was also produced locally in Islamic territories. New dyes, such as indigo from India, made textiles even more appealing. These changes gave new impetus to the textile industry.

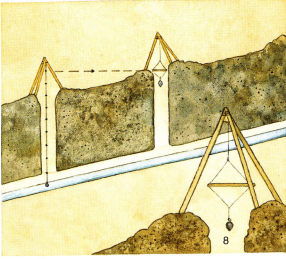

Miniature paintings from a 16th-century Persian dictionary showing (1) a peasant plowing a field with two buffalo, (2) a woman crushing grain, (3) an artisan forging a millstone with hammer and chisel, and (4) a peasant carding cotton.

5. This illustration from an Iraqi manuscript of 1237 shows ox driven fountain pumps in a garden in Baghdad.

6. Men building a *ganat,* a remarkable piece of hydraulic engineering invented by the Iranians

7. Countryside with *ganats,* as seen on the surface

8. A *ganat* seen in cross-section. Air shafts sunk at regular intervals allow the excavation and maintenance of an underground canal, which, reaching a deep source of water, supplies the water to irrigate the fields.

Glass vial from 9th-century Samarra

There were also new developments in writing materials. Chinese paper, made from hemp or flax, was now in use alongside papyrus from Egypt and parchment. A paper-making factory was erected in Baghdad in the 9th century, and it produced the paper used by the government in public administration.

Many of the articles produced by the artisans were so well crafted and decorated that they had considerable artistic merit. This was especially true of ceramics and glassware, which were inspired by the fine glass produced by Venetian glassmakers. Carpets, the necessary adjunct to nomadic life, became one of the most distinctive and valued products of artisans in the Muslim Middle East.

Right: A glassmaker in his workshop making fine pieces of glass
Center: A colored glass bottle from the 9th century

ISLAMIC EGYPT

The Islamic era brought new prosperity to Egypt, helping the country recover its ancient splendor, power, and cultural vigor. The golden age of Muslim Egypt began when the Abbasids appointed Ahmad ibn Tulun as governor of the territory. Ibn Tulun was the son of a Turkish slave who gained great honor at the court of Baghdad. He quickly proved a very able governor, with authority over an enormous territory that stretched beyond the borders of Egypt into Syria.

Ibn Tulun paid particular attention to organizing the army, since his authority depended to some extent on military strength. He tried to make sure that his soldiers were efficient, disciplined, and satisfied with their pay.

Ibn Tulun also devoted attention to the needs of the civilian population. Eventually, he refused to send the annual tribute to the Abbasid caliphs and instead used the money to develop Egypt's economy. He enriched the capital of al-Fustat by building a hospital, an aqueduct, and the great mosque that still bears his name to this day. He also built a new administrative capital, known as al-Qita'i, just to the northeast of al-Fustat. Through these actions, Ibn Tulun effectively declared his independence from Baghdad.

Ibn Tulun did not overlook the cultural welfare of the country. He gave his support to scholars, writers, artists, and scientists who immortalized the glory of his dynasty.

The Tulunids remained in power from 868 to 905, but the country began to decline during the reign of Ibn Tulun's son, Khumarawayh, who spent money lavishly, leaving the country with debts and reduced resources. Khumarawayh also escalated tensions with the Abbasids in Baghdad, who wanted to recover control of Egypt. To cement a new alliance with the Abbasids, Khumarawayh married off his daughter to the Abbasid caliph al-Mu'tadid.

Tulunid Egypt was sometimes beset by internal troubles and external pressures. These were largely attributable to certain groups of intellectuals and the *ulama*, who were the religious scholars of Islam. These learned men never concealed their sympathy for the caliphs of Baghdad, whom they regarded as the only legitimate heirs to the Prophet. These powerful religious leaders refused to accept the authority of the Tulunids, a family of Turkish origin.

Khumarawayh was assassinated by a slave, and the Abbasids drove his two sons from power. Egypt was then governed once again by viceroys, or governors, sent from Baghdad and loyal to the caliph. By now, however, the process of political disintegration and decentralization within the entire Abbasid Empire was well advanced, and Egypt soon became relatively independent again.

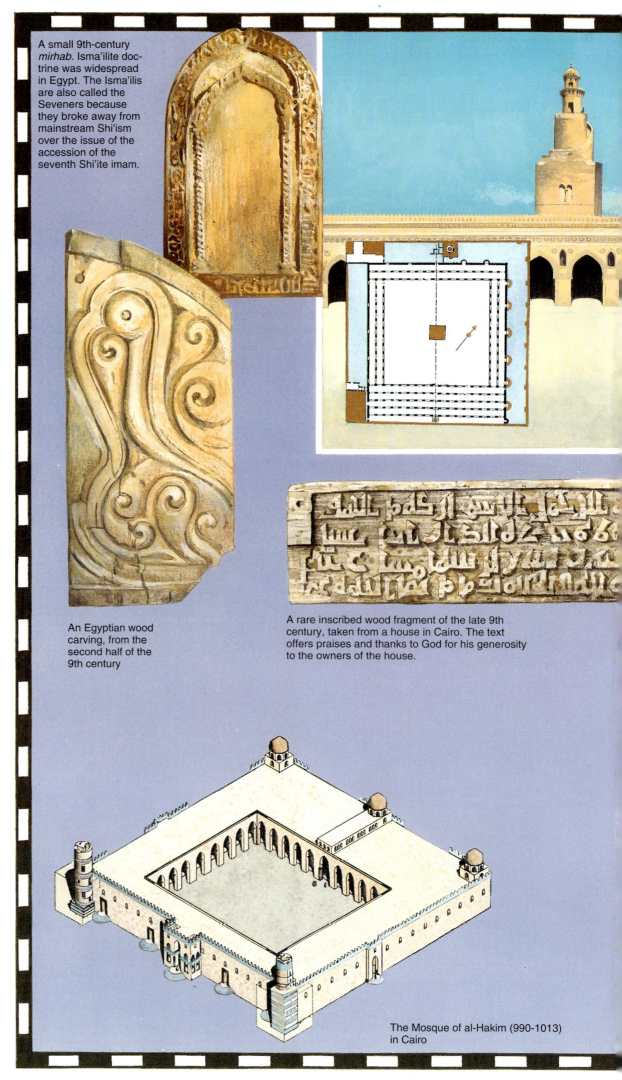

A small 9th-century *mirhab*. Isma'ilite doctrine was widespread in Egypt. The Isma'ilis are also called the Seveners because they broke away from mainstream Shi'ism over the issue of the accession of the seventh Shi'ite imam.

An Egyptian wood carving, from the second half of the 9th century

A rare inscribed wood fragment of the late 9th century, taken from a house in Cairo. The text offers praises and thanks to God for his generosity to the owners of the house.

The Mosque of al-Hakim (990-1013) in Cairo

In the foreground, above, is an Egyptian horseman wearing the characteristic uniform of the late 9th century. Behind the Egyptian is a Nubian infantryman of the 10th century.

Muhammad ibn Tughj was appointed governor of Egypt in 935. He followed a strategy similar to that of Ibn Tulun, and he too succeeded in asserting his independence. Ibn Tughj expanded his territory to take in the Sinai Peninsula and Syria. In Syria he obtained authority over Damascus.

On his death his two sons succeeded him. But Kafur, an advisor of exceptional ability, gained power as regent. Kafur thus exercised the highest authority as long as he was alive. For years, he battled successfully against rebellious tribes in Syria and fended off the Fatimid Muslims, who were trying to gain control over Egypt. When Kafur died, the region became vulnerable to new conquest.

Isma'ilis and Carmathians

After their split with orthodox, or Sunni Islam, the Shi'ites also broke into a number of smaller groups, or sects. The majority sect was that of the Twelvers, but there was also a sect called the Seveners, or Isma'ilis, which attracted many followers, especially in Egypt and North Africa.

The Isma'ilis were persecuted from the start for the extremist views they held. Isma'ilis regarded Ali and the imams who came after him as the only people with knowledge of the real inner meaning of the Koran. The Isma'ilis sent secret missions throughout the vast regions of the Islamic world to win new converts through their tireless preaching.

One of these Isma'ilis was Hamdan Qarmat, who started a new sect, the Carmathians, in the Persian Gulf area. The religious beliefs of the Carmathians are rather unclear to us today, but it seems that their social program included an egalitarian ideal. This may explain why this revolutionary movement was so popular with the masses who were discontented with the caliphal system.

The ferocity with which the Carmathians fought to assert their beliefs led to such violent battles that many regions were brought to the brink of civil war. After a brief period of success in the late 9th and early 10th centuries, the Carmathian movement began to decline, and within a few decades it disappeared from the scene altogether.

In the center of the page above is the Mosque of Ibn Tulun, which was built in Cairo in 876. It was built in the Abbasid architectural style of Samarra. The arcades are 410 feet long with slightly broken horseshoe arches.

Left: In front of the Mamluk dome and minarets is the Mosque of al-Aqmar. This mosque was built in 1125 and is considered one of the most important buildings in the urban development of Cairo. Although the facade aligns with the street, the interior is oriented toward Mecca.

The Mosque of al-Azhar was built in Cairo between 970 and 972, when the city was an active center of Isma'ili propaganda. When Egypt returned to Sunni control, the mosque retained its great prestige, becoming the seat of one of the leading Muslim theological schools.

The citadel of Aleppo was occupied by Saladin in 1189 and turned into a center of resistance against the Crusaders.

This late 10th-century pitcher was made of rock crystal during a period when the traditional designs of stone reliefs were translated into the finest glass works of art.

The remains of a 10th-century palace built in Libya, presumably as a residence for the caliph al-Mu'izz during his advance toward Cairo

This fortress was built 75 miles north of Damascus and close to the sea. Its foundations may date back to very ancient times. From 1142 to 1271, it was occupied by the soldier-monks of the order of St. John of Jerusalem, who turned it into an impregnable stronghold.

11th or 12th century Fatimid mausoleums in Cairo

- Maximum extent of the Islamic world in the 12th century
- Mainland route followed by the Crusader expeditions to the Holy Land

THE FATIMIDS AND SALADIN

The Fatimids, whose name derives from Fatima, the daughter of the Prophet Muhammad and the wife of Ali, belonged to the Isma'ilite sect of Shi'ites. They came to power through an extensive network of Isma'ili missionaries, who were very active in North Africa. In 910, the Fatimids successfully established a caliphate in Tunisia in opposition to the Abbasid caliphate in Baghdad. In 969 Gawar, general to the Fatimid caliph al-Mu'izz, invaded Egypt and took the country with little difficulty.

One of his first initiatives was to begin building a new capital still farther northeast of al-Fustat. The settlement was intended mainly for housing government offices and the military administration. He named the city al-Qahira, "the Victorious," which today is known in English as Cairo.

The Fatimids expanded their territory into Syria and beyond Damascus itself. Their influence reached the Arabian Peninsula, where they ruled over the holy cities of Mecca and Medina.

The Fatamids administered a powerful trading empire, and Cairo became a great cultural center and meeting place. As in all periods of prosperity, the arts flourished, encouraged by support from the government and from rich patrons.

During the late 11th and 12th centuries, the Fatimid dynasty lost, regained, and again lost some of its provincial territories and cities. Jerusalem was taken from the Fatimids by the Seljuk Turks in 1071. It was temporarily retaken by the Fatimids and held until the arrival of the Crusader armies, which occupied the Holy City in 1096. The Crusaders ultimately took all the Fatimid possessions in Palestine and even threatened Egypt itself.

Some of the small Crusader states created in the Holy Land survived for almost two centuries. Ultimately, the Crusaders were unable to withstand the great force of medieval Islam, and

An ivory horn from the 11th or 12th century

Below center: A ceramic plate from the first half of the 12th century. The plate shows a Coptic priest, reflecting the prosperity of the large native Christian population of Egypt in the Fatimid period. Today Copts (or Egyptian Christians) still account for about 6 percent of Egypt's population.

The Fatimid caliphs exercised religious tolerance in the areas they controlled. Jews and Christians could build their own places of worship, and monasteries were protected by the government. Non-Muslims held positions of high authority in the state.

This tolerance of other religions was lacking only during the caliphate of al-Hakim, between 966 and 1020. He ordered that many churches be razed, including the Church of the Holy Sepulcher in Jerusalem. Al-Hakim may well have been mentally unbalanced, using his power in strange ways. He alternated between acts of great generosity toward those in need and acts of gratuitous cruelty. In 1017, after experiencing a religious crisis, he declared himself the "dwelling place of the godhead." His mysterious disappearance in 1021 gave rise to the sect of the Druze.

Below: Crusaders surrendered to Saladin in the south tower of the citadel of Aleppo. The Crusaders themselves made far less impact on the Muslim world than they made on the West. In the eyes of Islam, the Christian knights were motivated solely by their desire to increase their territories and grow rich on the booty of war. They were regarded and fought by Muslims as traditional enemies. The position of native Christians in the Muslim world had always been subject to ups and downs.

The Abbasid caliphs were so weak by this period that they could do little but regard the Crusades as a local problem. For this reason the Muslim world was forced to rely on the armies of regional empires, like the Fatimids, to fight the Crusaders. The weight of war thus fell repeatedly on Egypt and on Syria. The Crusaders who occupied Edessa and Antioch were engaged first by local forces and their Kurdish allies.

Palestine came under Muslim control once again.

Saladin served originally as a Fatimid general and went on to replace the Fatimids with his own Ayyubid dynasty in 1171. In addition to being a great Islamic hero for defeating the Crusaders, Saladin restored Egypt to Sunni control. Although Saladin was an independent ruler, he paid nominal allegiance to the traditional Abbasid caliph in Baghdad. He died in Damascus, mourned by the common people as well as the nobility.

The Druze

The Druze take their name from al-Darazi, one of the most active Isma'ili missionaries of the Fatimid caliph al-Hakim. After al-Hakim's mysterious disappearance, al-Darazi preached the cult of al-Hakim in Syria and present-day Lebanon.

The Druze have always remained a segregated community with their own forms of worship and rituals. They are characterized by their refusal to seek or even accept converts. Little is known about their doctrine, but one of their beliefs is that there are only a limited number of souls in existence. Consequently, they believe in the transmigration of souls, or reincarnation.

THE SELJUK TURKS

A new stage in the history of the Muslim world began with the rise of the Seljuk Turks in Central Asia. The dynasty they established brought renewed unity and stability to an Islamic world divided politically and religiously.

The Turks were a warlike nomadic people who, with their conversion to Islam, changed the course of medieval history in the Middle East. The lands that stretched from Afghanistan to Syria soon came under their control.

The Seljuks were only one of numerous Turkish tribes that migrated west from the Steppes of Central Asia. From northern China to the plains of Russia, large confederations of nomadic peoples fought among themselves and plundered the settled populations, bringing ruin and devastation to the lands they crossed. In such an unstable world, the Turkish tribes found themselves pushed into the Islamic world where they began to settle and convert to Islam. They sought the relative peace, stability, and protection offered by the Muslim world. With the passing years, many of these nomadic tribes also welcomed the new faith, Islam.

The Seljuks stood out from the varied Turkish tribes with their superior military strength and strategy. Once they crossed the Oxus River, they continued westward until they conquered Baghdad. It was the Abbasid caliph himself, al-Qa'im, who summoned the Seljuk leader, Toghril Beg, into the city. Tired of being under the thumb of his Persian Buyid overlords, the caliph did not hesitate in recognizing the power of fellow Sunnis. The Seljuks ended Shi'ite power in Mesopotamia and helped reorganize and revitalize the basis of Sunni society.

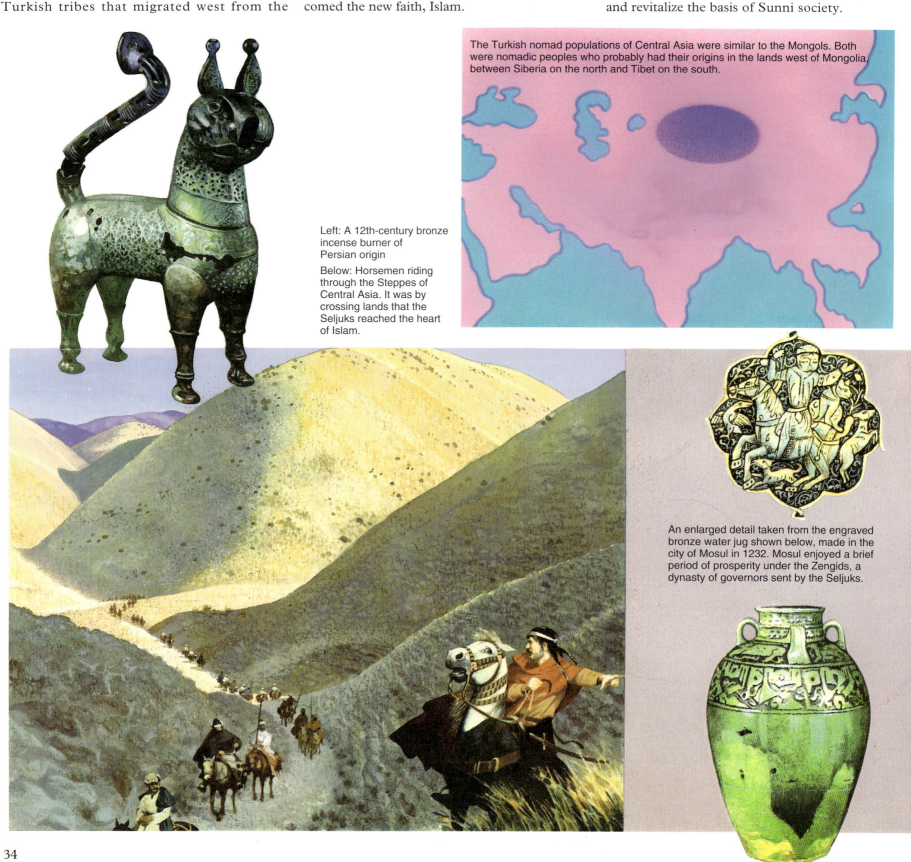

The Turkish nomad populations of Central Asia were similar to the Mongols. Both were nomadic peoples who probably had their origins in the lands west of Mongolia, between Siberia on the north and Tibet on the south.

Left: A 12th-century bronze incense burner of Persian origin

Below: Horsemen riding through the Steppes of Central Asia. It was by crossing lands that the Seljuks reached the heart of Islam.

An enlarged detail taken from the engraved bronze water jug shown below, made in the city of Mosul in 1232. Mosul enjoyed a brief period of prosperity under the Zengids, a dynasty of governors sent by the Seljuks.

The last Abbasid caliphs were unable to rule their large empire. They had to yield power to local governors, who were clamoring for autonomy. The Abbasid court itself was also riddled with corruption. Internal tensions became so acute that Iraq was plunged into civil war on several occasions. No fewer than five caliphs were assassinated during the decade 860 to 870.

The 10th century was a time of fierce and bloody religious fighting in the Muslim world. The weakness of the central government was apparent in its failure to prevent this religious strife. The period from 950 to 1050 is sometimes called "the Shi'ite century" by scholars.

The rise of the Seljuks put an end to this situation. The caliph did not hesitate in handing political authority over to the Turks. The Seljuk leaders took the title *sultan*, which comes from a word meaning "power." The Turkish princes recognized the religious authority of the caliph, and they were granted political power in exchange for the protection they gave to the caliph. Toghril Beg was granted the title "king of the East and the West," and he set about restoring the authority and prestige of the caliphate.

Two basic features of Seljuk power were the great importance they attached to military strength and their unwavering allegiance to the Sunni faith. The greatest of the Seljuk sultans were fighting men. They left administration to very capable civilians who organized a highly effective government. Social life and trade continued to follow patterns established through the centuries, and both benefited from the period of peace established by Turkish power.

The army owed its prestige and its successes in the field to the tactics adopted from the nomadic Turkish techniques. The Turks avoided frontal assaults in favor of skirmishes and swift attacks by their feared squadrons of bowmen mounted on horseback. They often faked retreats that drew their enemies into hostile countryside. There the Turks surrounded and slaughtered their foes.

In religious matters, the Seljuk century was characterized by a rejuvenation of orthodox Islam and a renewed commitment to the authority of the sunna. With the help of famous theologians such as al-Ghazali, who is honored throughout the Islamic world, and mystics who were now united and controlled through powerful fraternities, the return to tradition was not imposed by force but carried out with popular support. An important new institution established under the Seljuks was the *madrassa*, a mosque-school where young men were taught systematic theology. Graduates could teach in mosque-school or preach in a mosque. Many aspects of Seljuk culture were adopted by the rest of the Muslim world and long survived the dissolution of the Seljuk dynasty.

Seljuk power came to an end due to overexpansion and rivalry over succession to the sultanate. The vast extent of the Seljuk Empire inevitably led to problems in far-flung provinces. There was also mounting pressure from new invaders coming from the East.

The illustration below shows mounted bowmen shooting arrows over their shoulders. This feat was made possible by the use of a saddle of Mongolian design with a very low back.

Bottom right-hand corner: A guard and a drummer accompany a town crier as he announces new government directives imposed by the Seljuks.

Below left: This ceramic jar decorated with animals and writing comes from 12th-century Kurdistan.

Above: This bronze medallion from 12th-century Asia Minor is now in the Louvre Museum in Paris, France.

Below: A glazed jug with decorations in relief from 12th-century Persia

ISLAMIC SPAIN

The Arab occupation of Spain started as a simple raid, but the occupation became a lasting conquest, in which Spain was subject to the authority of the Umayyad caliphs. The land was given the Arabic name al-Andalus, a reminder of the period when Spain had been occupied by the Vandals. In 756 Muslim Spain became independent of the Abbasid caliphate. It came under the control of Abd al-Rahman, the only Umayyad prince to have escaped the massacres that followed the Abbasid Revolution. Al-Andalus was now called the emirate of Córdoba.

In 929 the emirate proclaimed itself the caliphate of Córdoba. The caliphate was named after the city of Córdoba, the new capital. By proclaiming its political independence, Islamic Spain removed itself from the sovereignty of Baghdad.

Muslims controlled the entire Iberian Peninsula, including the future kingdom of Portugal. Within a short time, Islamic Spain became a place of unrivaled luxury and cultural refinement. We can still marvel at the magnificent buildings and gardens built for the ruling Muslim princes in Granada. These structures had a style of architecture referred to in the West as Moorish, after the name Europeans gave to the Arabs who occupied Spain.

This corner of Europe was so permeated by Islamic culture that to this day there are reminders of the period. The fusion of two such profoundly different cultures, Western and Islamic, gave rise to a unique civilization in which three religions coexisted—Islam, Judaism, and Christianity. One aspect of cultural exchange, the translation of Latin texts into Arabic and vice versa, was the work of Jewish scholars in Toledo.

The Christians living in Spain under Muslim rule who had acquired Arab characteristics and culture came to be called Mozarabs. Magnificent 8th-century illustrated manuscripts bear witness to the birth of an Arabic-Christian literature. The Mozarabs were allowed to hold public office and were given positions of considerable importance. During the rule of al-Hakam (796-822), a Christian was even in command of the emir's bodyguard.

Al-Hakam's son, Abd al-Rahman II, was one of the most important rulers of Islamic Spain. He adopted the Abbasid form of administration and court procedure and initiated a series of

Left: A detail of the ruins of the Madinat al-Zahra, a city built on the outskirts of Córdoba by an-Nasir in the 10th century

Below: This illustration of an Arab and a Christian playing chess is taken from the 13th-century book *Libro des Ajedres*.

Right: On January 2, 1492, Muhammad XI (known in Spanish as Boabdil), the last Muslim ruler of Granada, handed over the keys of the city to the Catholic kings. This illustration is taken from a relief created by Felipe Biguerny in the royal chapel in Granada during the 16th century.

The Reconquest (see map below left)
1. The stages of the reconquest. Starting with the small kingdoms in the north of the Iberian Peninsula, the reconquest continued during the 10th to 12th centuries. The first stage was completed in the 12th century.
2. Islamic lands at the end of the 13th century

reforms that made him an important figure in the Muslim world. Abd al-Rahman enlarged and embellished the capital. He also instituted state manufacturing and government control over the production and distribution of certain basic goods.

Throughout centuries of Islamic rule, life in Spain was enriched by art and music. Córdoba became an important center of music, with a lute-making industry and a famous music conservatory.

This musical tradition was followed in the other great Andalusian cities. The musicians of Seville, Granada, and Toledo had great influence on the compositions of the future troubadours of Provence. This influence can be found in both the structure of their musical themes and the poetic compositions that accompanied them.

Christian Europe, however, never accepted the intrusion of Islam into Spain, and a process known as the reconquest began. The reconquest of Spain was led by rulers of the Christian kingdoms of Spain. Others joining in the fighting were French knights, militaristic religious orders, and merchants from Pisa and Genoa. What started as Christian raids on Muslim positions grew into extensive Crusades with the goal of winning Spain back for the Europeans.

The fortunes of the two sides fluctuated until the great victory of the Christian armies at Las Navas de Tolosa in 1212. The Almohad dynasty, which was then ruling North Africa and Spain, began to disintegrate. Muslim cities fell one after the other.

Córdoba surrendered to Ferdinand III of Castile in 1236, and the onslaught of the reconquest swarmed over Cádiz, which was taken in 1250. Islam retained its power only in Granada, resisting the Catholic kings until 1492.

The Alhambra—a residential palace with many fountains, gardens, and magnificent decorations of inlay, stuccowork, and tile—is a remarkable example of the refinement of the Muslims in Spain. The Alhambra was built in Granada during the reign of Yusuf I (1333-1354).

A section of an arched ceiling in the Mosque at Córdoba. The mosque became a Catholic cathedral. The building was extended to cover an area of about 900 feet by 515 feet. On the inside, a forest of 1,293 columns supported the vaulted ceilings. The mosque was lit with enormous lamps and lanterns made from Christian bronze bells.

This mosque in Kairouan, Tunisia, was originally built in 670 and rebuilt several times. It provides an example of Aghlabid architecture, which strongly influenced mosque-building in North Africa. Facing onto the courtyard is a covered portico resting on a series of columns. Its arcades surround the T-shaped central corridor that ends in a transept against the back walls.

This Aghlabid reservoir was built in the 9th century. It has a diameter of 420 feet.

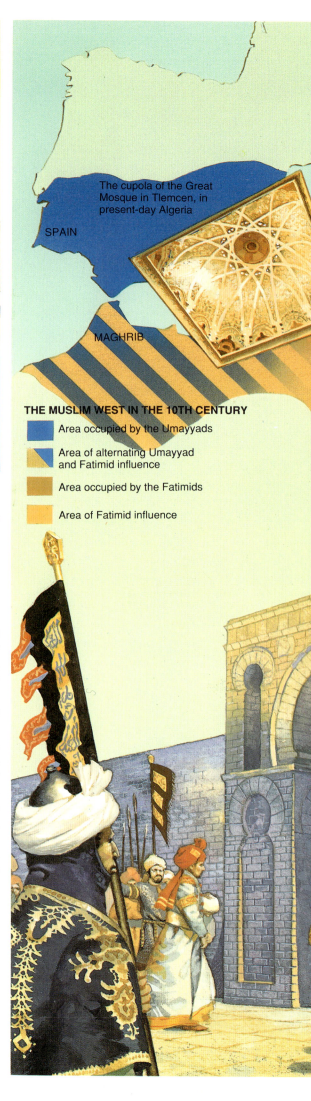

The cupola of the Great Mosque in Tlemcen, in present-day Algeria

THE MUSLIM WEST IN THE 10TH CENTURY
- Area occupied by the Umayyads
- Area of alternating Umayyad and Fatimid influence
- Area occupied by the Fatimids
- Area of Fatimid influence

THE MAGHRIB BEFORE THE ALMORAVIDS

The Arab world used the name *Maghrib* to designate the huge geographical area stretching from the Atlantic Ocean in the west to the Libyan border with Egypt in the east. The Maghrib included the former Roman province in Africa named Ifriqiyya, which had been taken by Musa ibn Nusayr in the earliest days of Islamic expansion. The actual meaning of the word *Maghrib* is "place of the sunset." This region to the north of the Sahara Desert is more closely associated with the civilizations of the Mediterranean world than with those of sub-Saharan Africa.

In the year 800, the governor of Ifriqiyya, Ibrahim ibn al-Aghlab, obtained independence for his province. He realized that the distance of his province from Baghdad would discourage the Abbasid caliphate from trying to stop his defection.

Muslim Sicily

Ibn al-Aghlab extended his power westward as far as Annaba, in present-day Algeria, and eastward as far as Barka, in present-day Libya. He encouraged maritime expeditions, both for piracy and conquest.

The Muslims seized Sicily when the island was in Byzantine possession. Without considering the consequences of his actions, the commander of the Byzantine fleet summoned Muslim ships to his aid during a war. The Muslims subsequently conquered the cities of Mazara del Valo, Palermo, and Syracuse in 876. Sicily now belonged entirely to the Muslims.

The era of Islamic control of Sicily was to prove one of the greatest periods in that island's history. Once again the island's fertile land was cultivated as it had been in classical antiquity. Muslim pirates based in Sicily obligated Pope John VIII to pay tribute to them rather than endure the continual devastation of the coasts and countryside of the papal state by marauding Muslim ships. Muslim princes became immensely wealthy. The princes were astute politicians, and they settled internal conflicts and sought to immortalize themselves by building fine monuments and new cities.

Unrest in the Maghrib

Aghlabid power waned in the Maghrib because of a violent Berber revolt fomented by the rival Fatimid dynasty. The Fatimids deposed the last Aghlabid ruler in 909 and used the Maghrib to launch their conquest of Egypt.

The Muslim states in the western Mediterranean began to decline in the 11th century. Italian city-states, such as Genoa and Venice, competed successfully with Muslim traders and

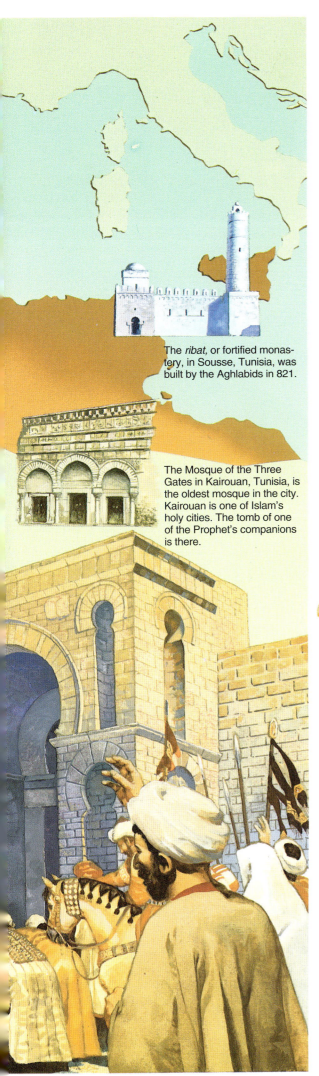

The *ribat*, or fortified monastery, in Sousse, Tunisia, was built by the Aghlabids in 821.

The Mosque of the Three Gates in Kairouan, Tunisia, is the oldest mosque in the city. Kairouan is one of Islam's holy cities. The tomb of one of the Prophet's companions is there.

Left: The large illustration shows a Fatimid caliph entering the Great Mosque of Mahdiyya, built in 916. The mosque entrance, which recalls Roman triumphal arches, has been rebuilt several times.

soon dominated the sea. At the same time, Norman armies from France reconquered Sicily. Local Christians welcomed the Normans as deliverers from the "infidel" Muslims.

The Normans drove the Muslims out of Sicily and, in 1090, also reconquered Malta. The Norman conquests caused many Muslim intellectuals and members of the highest social classes to flee to North Africa. But the Normans briefly pressed on into Africa, too, where they seized the cities of Tripoli and Kairouan.

At almost the same time, the Maghrib once again was torn by the revolts of rival Berber clans. Two important groups of Berbers, the Sanhaja and the Zenaga, were in frequent conflict. The Sanhaja supported the Fatimids, and a Sanhaja family, the Zirids, governed Ifriqiyya for the Fatimid dynasty. The rival clan of the Banu Hammad controlled Algeria.

The Zirids enjoyed great prosperity until one of their princes, al-Mu'izz, rebelled against Fatimid control. The Egyptian caliph decided to punish his rebel vassal by taking harsh measures. He ordered the devastation of Ifriqiyya by fierce Bedouin tribes from Arabia. These tribes caused such havoc that the country fell into economic ruin and anarchy for many years. The Zirids could find no place of refuge except in the coastal cities, where they turned to piracy.

This livelihood brought about the Zirid's eventual ruin because the pirate raids provoked reprisals by the Genoese and Pisan merchant fleets. Exasperated by continual Muslim pirate raids, the Italians succeeded in striking the Zirid capital, al-Mahdiyya. The city subsequently fell into the hands of the Normans, who ruled there until the arrival of the Almohads in 1159.

The Almohads had already destroyed the power of the Banu Hammad of Tripoli in 1152, and the new dynasty's relations with the Italian city-states were very good. There was now a period of relative peace in North Africa.

Shown below are three types of pillars used in Islamic architecture:
A. Byzantine capital. Earlier architectural elements, Roman or Byzantine, were frequently used in buildings in the Maghrib.
B. Arabic capital of the 13th through 15th centuries
C. Arabic capital of the 10th and 11th centuries

The Madrassa of al-Attarin, or "perfume sellers," was built in Fez between 1323 and 1325. The *madrassa* stands in a southern quarter of the city that is reserved for perfume makers, hence its name.

THE MAGHRIB: THE ALMORAVIDS AND THE ALMOHADS

Above: A detail of the wooden gateway to the Bou Inaniya Madrassa in Fez, Morocco. Attached to the mosques, *madrassas* were schools of higher learning where theology, law, and Muslim religious sciences were taught.

The 11th century was a troubled period in the history of the Maghrib. A serious economic crisis was caused by the devastation wrought by Arab nomads. Religious life was also weakened by divisions between Islamic sects.

One Berber tribe, the Almoravids of Ibn Yasin, was eventually strong enough to gain control over the area. Coming from the Western Sahara, the Almoravids acted much like an Islamic version of the Crusaders. Trained in fortified religious retreats (*ribats*), they set out first to subdue the surrounding Berber tribes. They next turned to the southerly kingdom of Ghana, which they conquered in 1076.

The successor of Ibn Yasin was Yusuf Ibn Tashfin, who made Marrakesh the capital of his new kingdom. At the same time, the power of the Almoravids reached as far as central Algeria. Almoravid expansion stretched into the Iberian Peninsula, where the Almoravids were initially summoned in 1086 by the local Muslim rulers to help fight King Alfonso VI of Aragon.

The refined Spanish world, which the Almoravids helped save, was ultimately fatal to their dynasty. Beguiled by the luxury and riches of the court of Córdoba, the Almoravids soon lost their religious fervor. Jealousies, intrigues, and jostling for power led to the downfall of the Almoravid dynasty in less than a century.

The Muslim West was again united into a single kingdom by another Berber tribal confederation, the Almohads, that came down from the mountains of Morocco to conquer the Maghrib. They were led by Ibn Tumart, a great commander and a fervent Muslim, who was determined to restore the purity of early Islam in West Africa and Spain. In his reforming zeal, Ibn Tumart proclaimed himself to be the Mahdi. The Mahdi was a figure connected originally to Shi'ite tradition, a long-awaited kind of messiah whose interpretation of Islamic laws and traditions would be beyond question.

In his role as Mahdi, Ibn Tumart reorganized Muslim government. He set up a council of ten wise men to aid him in running the country, and he established a much larger group of representatives from the various tribes to protect the interests of the whole community.

Ibn Tumart's favorite disciple was Abd al-Mu'min ibn Ali, a man more concerned with expanding Almohad territory than with reforming the government. Within about 15 years, starting from 1130, he gained possession of all the Maghrib.

As the Turks and the Kurds in the East supported a revival of Sunni Islam, so did Abd al-Mu'min in the West. This revival was further supported by Sufi mystics. These pious men abandoned everything to offer their lives to Islam. In North Africa these mystics were called marabouts. They were regarded by other Muslims as saints.

Below: The Hassan Tower in Rabat, Morocco, imitates the Great Towers of the Kutubiyya in Marrakesh. The decoration of the Hassan Tower is different on each side. Its minaret and adjacent mosque remain unfinished. If its minaret had been finished, it would have been one of the largest mosques in the Muslim world. Its base alone measures 145 feet, which, considering the proportions of the Almohad minarets, would have meant a full height of about 260 feet.

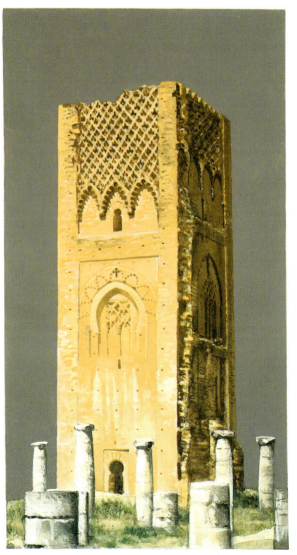

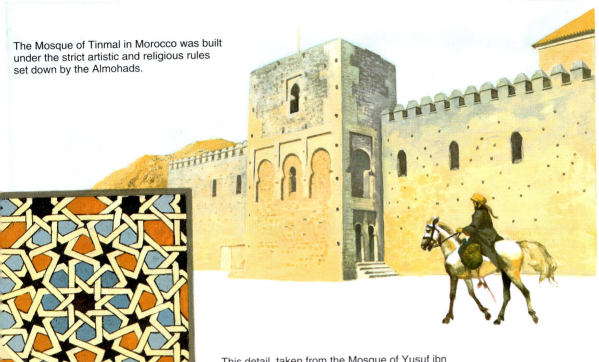

The Mosque of Tinmal in Morocco was built under the strict artistic and religious rules set down by the Almohads.

This detail, taken from the Mosque of Yusuf ibn Tashfin in Tlemcen, Algeria, shows the intricate geometric inlays created in conformity with the rules of Islamic abstract art.

The State

The Almoravid state had a strongly centralized government. Zealous Almoravid officials ordered that all of North Africa be measured so that a tax payable by each province might be calculated.

Despite adopting excellent methods of government, the Almoravid state began to lose power during the second half of the 13th century. Its princes were no longer able to contain the trouble caused by some of the turbulent Berber tribes in the Maghrib. Spain was yielding to the pressure of the Christian reconquest.

Left: The cupola in the *mihrab* of the Great Mosque in Tlemcen, Algeria, a city founded by the Almoravids in the 11th century

The illustration below shows dyers at work in the city of Fez. Many Islamic cities were planned around the activities of different industries or activities.

A street fountain in Fez shows rich decoration and skilled workmanship. In countries where water was a precious commodity, rich benefactors would win over the support of the people by erecting large and beautiful public water fountains.

Shown at the bottom of this page is the Torre de Oro, which was erected in the 12th century as part of the fortified walls of Seville, Spain.

THE IMPACT OF THE MONGOLS ON THE MUSLIM WORLD

The name *Mongol* designates a Central Asian people originating in the northeastern part of present-day Mongolia. The Mongols made an indelible mark on the history of the world.

The Mongols traditionally lived in nomadic tribes with no stable or united state. It was in the age of Temujin, the great Genghis Khan, that the Mongols became famous in the annals of the great empires of both the East and the West.

In 1206 Temujin assumed the title of Great Khan, or "universal sovereign," during an assembly of Mongol nobles over whom he successfully imposed his authority. He organized a highly efficient and strictly disciplined army. The army's particular strength lay with its extremely swift, mounted bowmen. The Mongol armies' strategies included attacking an enemy's flanks, encirclement, and feigned retreats.

The Mongols of Genghis Khan soon began to attack the civilizations beyond the Central Asian Steppes, starting with northern China. After sacking this region, they turned westward to the Caucasus Mountains and Volga River regions, employing artillery and other Chinese military techniques they had acquired.

Genghis Khan died in 1227, but his successors carried on the work he had begun. The Mongol leader, Ogödöi, pushing eastward, completed the conquest of northern China and advanced as far as Korea. In the West he laid waste to Poland and Hungary and reached the Adriatic Sea.

A third advance signaled the devastating impact of the Mongol hordes on the Muslim world. The new leader, Kublai Khan, achieved complete dominion over China and then directed his brother Möngke Hülegü toward Baghdad. In 1258 Möngke Hülegü conquered Iran.

Baghdad itself was taken in 1258; it was sacked and pillaged for a whole week. The caliph and all his household were massacred. The Islamic world suddenly found it had lost the city that for centuries had been the symbol of its splendor. Baghdad, as the seat of the caliphate, had been a common point of reference for all Sunni Muslims, even if its political supremacy was largely a fiction.

The Mongols did not stop at Baghdad. They attacked Damascus, which fell in 1260. They would have advanced farther if the Mamluk dynasty, firmly established in Egypt and Syria, had not fought so strenuously to drive the enemy out of Syria.

The Mamluks proved that the Mongols were not invincible, as the terrorized populations who had been subjected to their fearsome raids believed. However, the Mongols certainly had tremendous courage and equally remarkable powers of endurance. Their savagery and fearlessness helped feed the legends that surrounded them.

The Mongols invaded the Middle East as part of the Great Khan's vision of a world empire under his control. The sensational success and speed of the Mongols' conquests increased their ambitions and convinced their commanders that dreams of ruling the world were possible.

The Mongol khans chose Peking as their primary residence, leaving the provinces in the hands of governor-princes. Eventually, however, the Mongol Empire began to divide. The khanate (kingdom) of Persia was created, for example, with its first capital in Tabriz. The khanate of Kashgar was also created in modern Afghanistan.

The Islamic world ultimately managed to recover from this incredible upheaval, but the long-term cost of the Mongol invasions was high for the eastern Islamic world. Mesopotamia was so utterly defeated and demoralized that it never again played the leading role within the Muslim world as it had for centuries.

Another Mongol invasion took place in about 1360. It was conducted with even more savagery than the previous assaults. The new Mongol invaders, however, had already converted to Islam. With characteristic ardor, they were to become the most staunch defenders of Islamic law.

In the center of the opposite page is a miniature painting taken from a manuscript page of *The Universal History*, written by Rashid ad-Din in the 14th century. The painting shows the Mongol armies attacking Baghdad.

The Mongols surged into Baghdad and caused deep shock throughout the Islamic world. Never before had the city, the great symbolic capital of the Islamic world, fallen to non-Muslim invaders. Islam was no longer invincible if a foreign infidel enemy could succeed in wiping out the caliphate and destroying the city that had represented Islamic prestige for so long.

Above the painting of the Mongols invading Baghdad is an illustration of 13th-century funerary towers near Lake Van in Asia Minor.

Far right: The Mausoleum of Zubaydah was built in Baghdad in the 13th century. Zubaydah was the wife of the ruler Harun al-Rashid. The mausoleum is a polygonal structure; its cupola is almost a tower.

The illustrations on the bottom of this page show the following: a woman working on a traditional Persian loom; fragments of wool carpet with stylized birds, taken from the Mosque of 'Ala al-Din, built in Konya during the 12th century.

Carpets of Turkish origin have a large central field with geometric or stylized animal motifs and a border with small abstract or calligraphic decorations. The preferred colors are red, green, and many shades of blue.

The Mongols introduced new decorative motifs of Chinese origin, such as chrysanthemum flowers, clouds, and dragons.

The main entrance of a *madrassa* in Asia Minor

A bronze drum with engraved decorations. The drum was probably made during the 12th century in Persia.

1. Where the Mongols originated
2. The Mongol Empire in 1206
3. The Mongol Empire in the 14th century
4. Vassal states of the Mongols
5. Routes taken by the armies of Genghis Khan

An early 13th-century Persian glazed ceramic tile with calligraphic decoration in relief. Long panels of these tiles covered the walls of the mosque in Mashhad.

This hand-warmer in perforated bronze with silver inlays was made in Syria sometime between 1264 and 1269.

A 13th-century bronze vessel for grinding from Persia

TAMERLANE

Timur Lenk (Timur the Lame), known in the West as Tamerlane, was a military leader of Turkish-Mongolian background. He claimed descent from the great Genghis Khan. Tamerlane was so ruthless and cruel to his enemies that his deeds became well known. For example, he was said to have marked the path of his cavalry with piles of heads taken from his defeated enemies.

Tamerlane was determined to accomplish the dream of a world empire left unfinished by Genghis Khan. To accomplish this goal, he brought devastation and destruction to the western part of the Mongol Empire. He subjugated the khanates of Persia and Kashgar then led other expeditions, invading Russia, India, and Central Asia.

Tamerlane was a Muslim, and he fought in the name of Sunni Islam. He mercilessly persecuted the Shi'ites and followers of religions outside Islam.

Tamerlane's barbaric treatment of his enemies contrasted with his encouragement of science and the arts, especially in his capital city of Samarkand. He made Samarkand a political and cultural center once more.

Tamerlane died in 1405 after a 36 year reign, while he was preparing a large expedition against the khan of China. This last campaign was to have fulfilled his dream of creating a universal Islamic Empire.

The Islamic world survived the Mongol onslaught largely because the Mongols were not generally very concerned with religion. The other Mongol invaders, with exceptions such as Tamerlane, never openly sided with any of the different sects or movements within Islam. Lacking a strong unified religious tradition of their own, the Mongols quickly assimilated the religions of the areas they conquered.

From the institutional viewpoint, Mongol administration took on some features of classical Islamic government. At the same time, the Mongols certainly brought great changes to the heart of the Islamic world. The most notable change was the further decline in caliphal authority.

From their contact with Chinese traditions, the Mongols "imported" into the Middle East new methods of taxation. They also attempted to introduce paper money in place of coins of precious metal. The attempt failed.

Right: In Samarkand visitors walk among the mausoleums reserved for members of the ruling dynasty.

Below: This large bronze cauldron made for Tamerlane in Samarkand in the early 15th century is one of the best-known works of Islamic metallurgy.

The post-Mongol era began with the rise of an important new force in Asia Minor. Tamerlane conquered Ankara in 1402 and momentarily halted the rise of a new confederation of Turkoman tribes, who were known as the Ottomans. This new state had already shown its power by unifying Anatolia. Although the Ottomans did not initially have an organized state structure in the beginning, they soon became the core of a major new Islamic Empire that would lead the Islamic world for centuries.

From the beginning of the 13th century, Konya, an important Muslim city in Anatolia, was frequented by the leading Islamic scholars. The Iranian Jalal al-Din ar-Rumi died and was buried there in 1273. Ar-Rumi was one of Islam's greatest mystics as well as a great Persian poet. His sepulcher is still visited by thousands of pilgrims every year.

Although the Turks adopted the Muslim religion, they kept their own language. They used Arabic and Persian only for matters concerning religion or diplomatic relations. Turkish was used for administrative purposes and literature. As the Ottoman Turks consolidated power during the 13th century, the Turkish language inspired a wealth of poetry, narrative, and biographies of holy men.

Below left: A Turkish tomb in the area where Tamerlane's power was most widespread. These tombs recall the shape of the tents used by nomadic shepherds. The landscape in the background is typical of the Central Asian Steppes.

Below: A Mongol bowman. Tamerlane's troops were composed of Mongols and Turkomans.

Left: From the top of the minaret, a muezzin, or prayer announcer, intones praises to God at set hours and calls the faithful to prayer five times a day.

Below: The courtyard of the Madrassa of Sultan Hasan in Cairo. Completed in 1362, this building has the tallest minarets in Cairo and resembles a mighty fortress.

THE MAMLUKS

Overreliance on slave soldiers was as costly for the Ayyubids as it had been for the Abbasid caliphs before them. As these slave soldiers, known as Mamluks in Arabic, became more powerful, they took advantage of divisions over succession within the Ayyubid House to seize power altogether. The Mamluks employed by the Ayyubids were brought to Egypt from Central Asia. After extensive military training, these slaves were freed. They still owed their allegiance to their former masters, however. The first truly independent Mamluk leader was the legendary Baybars, who in 1260 started the Mamluk Empire.

The Mamluks showed remarkable military skill at a time when the eastern Muslim world faced serious military threats from both the Crusaders and the Mongols. Under pressure from the Mamluks, the European Crusaders lost Antioch in 1268 and Tripoli in 1289. In 1291 they lost Acre, their last stronghold in Palestine.

It was also in the 13th century that the Mamluks faced the advancing Mongols, who several times laid waste to parts of Syria but were unable to overcome the Egyptian forces. Syria became a bastion against invaders from the East and the eastern border of the Mamluk sultanate. At the same time, the power of the Ottomans was growing in Asia Minor, but it was not until the 16th century that they were strong enough to bring an end to Mamluk power. Until 1516, there was a rough balance of power between the Ottomans and the Mamluks in the Middle East.

Military power lay in the hands of a military oligarchy led by a sultan who rose to power based on his cunning and the strength of his allies. The state was run like a great army, and its strictly disciplined officials were trained in the barracks of Cairo and organized into a rigid hierarchy.

War, however, was not the only feature of Mamluk rule. Commercial activity increased as Egypt continued in its role as the center for trade between the Indian Ocean and the Mediterranean Sea. This brought new prosperity to the cities of Beirut, Damascus, Aleppo, and above all, Cairo. The state profited enormously from this lively trade. It maintained a monopoly over essential goods, and it enforced price controls. The Mamluk period was a golden age of Islamic art and architecture in Egypt. Cairo in the 14th and 15th centuries was one of the greatest cities in the world.

Cohesion between the ruling Turkish Mamluks and the Egyptian masses was ensured by a common faith. The Mamluks maintained strict adherence to Sunni Islam. In fact, the Mamluks, like the Ayyubids before them, saw themselves as the restorers of Sunni orthodoxy after two centuries of Shi'ite Fatimid rule.

The Mamluks proclaimed themselves defenders of the holy places of Islam. They showed their devotion by sending to Mecca every year beautiful embroidered cloth covers, known as *kiswa*, for the Ka'aba in Mecca. The Mamluks welcomed to Cairo the few surviving Abbasids who escaped

A picture of an Egyptian riverboat of the 15th century made of animal hide

This bronze basin was made in a Cairo workshop between 1220 and 1230.

the Mongol massacres. These survivors were honored and established as caliphs, with religious authority but no real political power. In turn, this puppet Abbasid caliphate provided the Mamluks with a greater measure of political legitimacy.

Religious life was vigorous. The Mamluks protected the Sufis, Islamic mystics who were regarded with suspicion by traditional Islamic scholars. Sufi groups and pious institutions proliferated, each run according to its own rules.

The world of culture saw a new impetus in literature and the figurative arts. One distinctive feature of artistic expression in the Mamluk centuries was the beauty and opulence that characterized Mamluk buildings. The architectural and decorative elements they used gave rise to a distinctive style. Many masterpieces of Mamluk architecture still survive in Cairo to this day.

In the world of letters there were two main developments. On the one hand, monumental encyclopedic works were written, among which were great manuals for the guidance and training of state officials. On the other hand, a new popular literature in the romantic tradition developed. Egyptian puppet theaters provided the only form of traditional theatrical representation in Islamic countries.

The Decline of the Mamluks

The powerful Mamluk Empire was defeated by external enemies. It bowed beneath the pressure of Portuguese expansion into the Red Sea and Ottoman invasions from the north. In 1517 the Turks established themselves in Cairo.

Meanwhile, a new era had begun. With the great geographical discoveries across the Atlantic Ocean and the sailing expeditions around the Cape of Good Hope, Egypt, and other countries circling the Mediterranean began to decline as Europeans redirected the vital Indian Ocean trade around southern Africa.

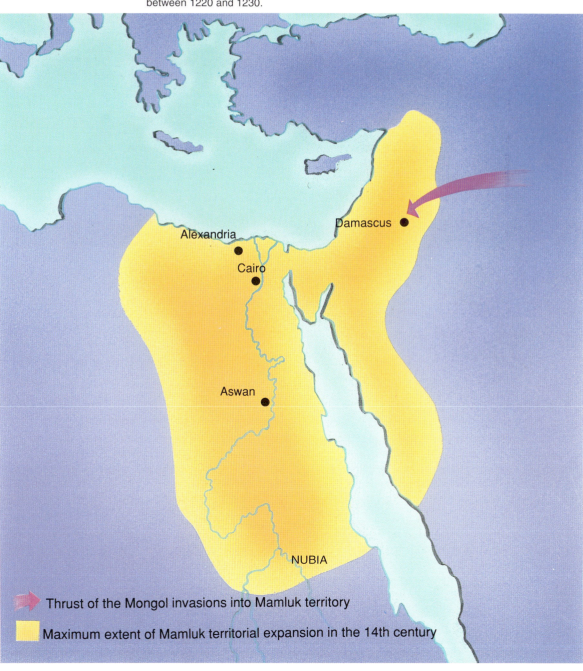

1. The Turks and Mongols originally came from the same regions in Central Asia, and they employed similar military tactics and arms. Tamerlane's Mongols succeeded in gaining the upper hand over the Ottomans, but his death signaled the end of the Mongol threat and gave the Ottomans the opportunity to extend their power.

2. Opposite page: Two high janissary officials in their distinctive dress uniform of the second half of the 16th century. They are holding special quivers and bows. An ordinary soldier is standing between the two officials.

3. The Green Mosque in Bursa, Turkey, where the tombs of the first Ottoman sultans are located. In 1326 Bursa was the capital of the new empire and an important commercial center where Oriental silks mingled with Arabian spices.

This steel helmet is ornamented with silver. The helmet was made around the year 1500 and bears the mark of an Istanbul arms manufacturer.

THE OTTOMANS

The founder of the Ottoman dynasty was Osman (Uthman). The Ottomans were only one of many Turkish peoples driven to the West by the Mongol invasions. They settled in a territory along the Seljuk frontier close to Constantinople. Their first capital was the city of Bursa.

Osman and his son Orhan pursued a shrewd and careful expansionist policy. They awarded newly conquered lands to subordinates in exchange for an obligation to supply soldiers for Ottoman military expeditions. In this way Osman and his son built up a large, motivated army, organized by Orhan himself.

Ottoman expansion continued at the expense of the Byzantine Empire. Nicaea and Nicomedia came under Ottoman rule, as did Pergamum in 1336. Ottoman power reached the coasts of the Aegean Sea and was soon felt in the Mediterranean. The coasts of Eastern Europe also began to fall prey to Ottoman raids.

The continuous Turkish expansion into Europe was undoubtedly helped by divisions among the European powers. The Venetians, Austro-Hungarians, Byzantines, Genoese, Serbs, and Bulgars were rivals in southeastern Europe, and they fought each other as often as they fought the Turks.

In 1396 the Ottomans began a series of unremitting attacks on the Byzantine Empire. Constantinople, the empire's capital, came under siege. Only the advance of Tamerlane into Asia Minor temporarily distracted Ottoman forces from Constantinople.

Tamerlane defeated the Ottomans, but he did not bring a permanent halt to their rise. Although their empire was split up, and they had to pay tribute for every conquest, the prestige of the Ottoman dynasty was not seriously damaged.

In 1414 Muhammad I, having eliminated his rivals, remained the only heir to the sultanate. Muhammad I successfully continued the expansionist strategy of his predecessors.

The Byzantine Empire continued to crack under Turkish pressure. In 1451, the Byzantine Empire collapsed as the Ottomans seized the city of Constantinople (known today as Istanbul).

The Army

Ottoman military power developed over a period of about 100 years, reaching its height in the 16th century. The standing army consisted

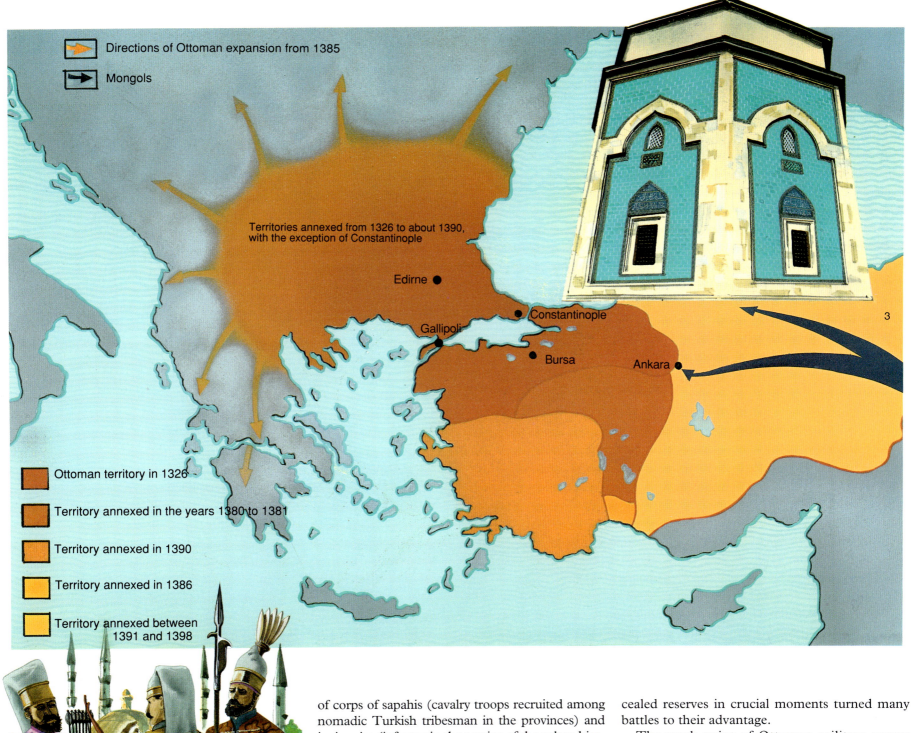

of corps of sapahis (cavalry troops recruited among nomadic Turkish tribesman in the provinces) and janissaries (infantry in the service of the sultan himself). The sapahis and janissaries were in addition to several contingents of irregulars.

The army's power rested with the janissaries, or "new troops." This corps, formed during the sultanate of Murad I, consisted of young men recruited by force exclusively from the sons of Christian families living in Turkish lands. These young men were educated and instructed in accordance with the principles of Islam. They were showered with gold and with honors, and they became genuinely faithful to the sultans. They were essentially Mamluks. Janissaries were not permitted to marry, and they observed a harsh discipline. They carried a white flag with verses from the Koran embroidered on it in silver thread. Their lives were devoted entirely to the sultan and to Islam.

The great strength of the Ottoman army lay in its numbers and its strategy. The Ottomans also used mounted bowmen in the Mongol tradition, and their strategy of bringing up carefully concealed reserves in crucial moments turned many battles to their advantage.

The weak point of Ottoman military power was the fleet. The Ottomans, coming from the Steppes of Central Asia, had no maritime traditions. They had no seafaring experience to rely on when they tried to tackle the Mediterranean, and they had few reliable ports outside their territories. Their fleet often proved inadequate and a costly waste of manpower and equipment.

Over the years the Turkish fleet grew more experienced. From the middle of the 16th century onward, on the orders of Suleiman the Magnificent (1522-1566), the fleet became completely independent of the rest of the military forces. This was due, in part, to the enterprising ex-pirate Khayr al-Din, called Barbarossa, the great admiral of Algiers. Barbarossa funded his navy without drawing directly on the imperial treasury. Instead, he collected tribute, or protection money, from the province of Algiers and from many Mediterranean islands. He received additional funds from the customs duties collected at major ports, such as Alexandria in Egypt.

THE FALL OF CONSTANTINOPLE AND THE SPLENDOR OF ISTANBUL

Muhammad II, "the Conqueror," succeeded his father Murad. Muhammad II was determined to incorporate into his empire the territories of states along the Ottoman frontiers.

His first target was Constantinople. To make certain no other power would attack the Turkish forces from the sea, he built a fortified blockade at the narrowest part of the Bosporus Strait. He wanted to prevent any fleets from coming to Constantinople's rescue.

Muhammad II then organized the siege of the great walled city using large numbers of men and such an impressive artillery force that it amazed chroniclers of the time. The Venetians and the Genoese tried to help Constantinople but to no avail. On May 29, 1453 the besieged city finally surrendered to the Turks. Ottoman troops poured into the city and sacked and plundered it for three days.

After the Turks had secured Constantinople, Muhammad II entered the city. He allowed the Christians to keep their faith and placed them under the protection of their patriarchs, or church leaders. Many Christian inhabitants decided to remain in the city.

Great numbers of Muslims from every part of the empire immigrated to Constantinople, and the city's population grew immensely. The

Left: A portrait of Muhammad painted in the late 15th century by the court painter Sinan Bey

Right: An exterior view of St. Sophia in Istanbul. The interior has a great central nave beneath a cupola measuring 102 feet, and semi-cupolas of the same diameter in front of and behind the central nave.

Below: The Ottomans used artillery in the final siege of Constantinople. European artillery experts helped the Ottomans build the cannons used to capture the Byzantine capital. One of these cannons was 26 feet long and could fire a projectile weighing over 1,000 pounds.

Muslims were induced to come by the ruling authorities, who wanted the old capital of the Byzantine Empire filled with the splendor of Islamic culture.

The name of the city was soon changed to Istanbul, a corruption of the Greek phrase *els ten polin*, "into the city," it having been called simply "the city" in Byzantine circles. Within a few years, Istanbul's appearance changed considerably. Marvelous new buildings replaced old wooden structures that had vanished in dreadful fires that periodically raged in Istanbul.

The 16th-century builders skillfully combined Byzantine architecture with the traditional Islamic approaches, thereby creating a new style. Muhammad II visited the famous church of St. Sophia soon after his armies took the city. The church had been built by Anthemius of Tralles and Isidorous of Miletus at the order of the emperor Justinian the Great. The sultan ordered its conversion into a Muslim mosque. The building that resulted from the alterations made by Muslim architects and artists became the model for future Ottoman constructions.

Another Byzantine building put to new use was the Basilica of St. Irene, seat of the Ecumenical Council of 381. The basilica was situated within the area occupied by the sultan's palace, so this ancient church was transformed into an arsenal for the janissaries.

Istanbul was carefully planned. Empty spaces around buildings of major importance, such as mosques, palaces, and baths, were filled with courts and rows of trees, laid out in a regular pattern. The overall effect was a city of carefully planned districts.

Muhammad II decided to build his royal palace on the site of the ancient Roman acropolis, which existed many centuries before the city was transformed by the Roman emperor Constantine. The acropolis was on a magnificent site overlooking the Sea of Marmara and the Bosporus. Today the palace bears the name Topkapi, but when it was completed it was known simply as the New Palace.

The palace was not actually a single structure but consisted of a number of detached buildings, each with different functions. The various buildings were constantly extended and altered. In the tradition of the ancient palaces of the Roman emperors, Topkapi accommodated thousands of people.

In the 16th century the New Palace's kitchen staff alone numbered more than 1,100 people. The staff produced daily meals for a court of about 5,000 people. Double that number of people could be served on special occasions, such as festivals.

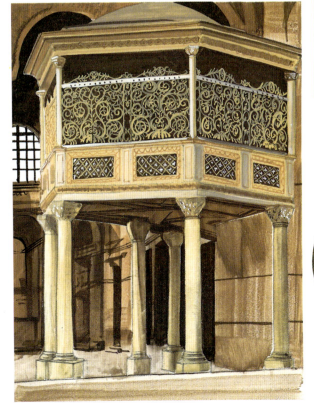

FROM A TURKISH CHRONICLE OF THE TIME

The Capture of Constantinople

...And as the river which leaves the Bosporus spreads out into a great sea, so the victorious soldiers of the Sultan, helped by Fortune, entered into the city through the arched gate, bringing down battle and terror on the heads of the unbelievers, and spread out through the city like a corrupting substance. And inside the city, which is greater than it is possible to imagine, the wicked infidels fled screaming before the mass of the Faithful.

...Then they dragged the infidel prince out of the palace, and out of the houses of the rich they dragged furniture and gold and silver vases, precious stones, jewels, and cloths of every kind, in such quantities that it seemed as if the earth itself was giving up its treasures....

Gold and silver could be bought for the price of copper and tin. In this way, through these precious things, many people raised themselves from the depths of poverty to extraordinary wealth.

Before St. Sophia

As he was visiting the many palaces, the wide streets, the markets of this ancient metropolis ... the sultan wished to admire the church that bears the name of Aya Sofya, a wonder of Heaven.... It is a mighty edifice, so great that to climb to the top, which is like the sky, you need to be immune to heights. There is nothing like it in the world.... But, as is inevitable with all man's creations, the buildings that surround the church are in ruins, just as are the envied palaces of those on whom fate once smiled....

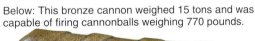

Below: This bronze cannon weighed 15 tons and was capable of firing cannonballs weighing 770 pounds.

Left: The sultan's open gallery, or loggia, in St. Sophia

OTTOMAN SUPREMACY IN THE ISLAMIC WORLD

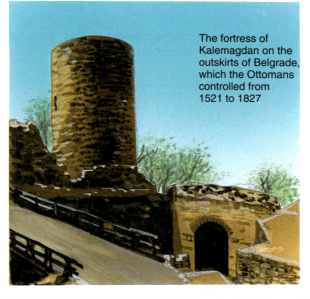

The fortress of Kalemagdan on the outskirts of Belgrade, which the Ottomans controlled from 1521 to 1827

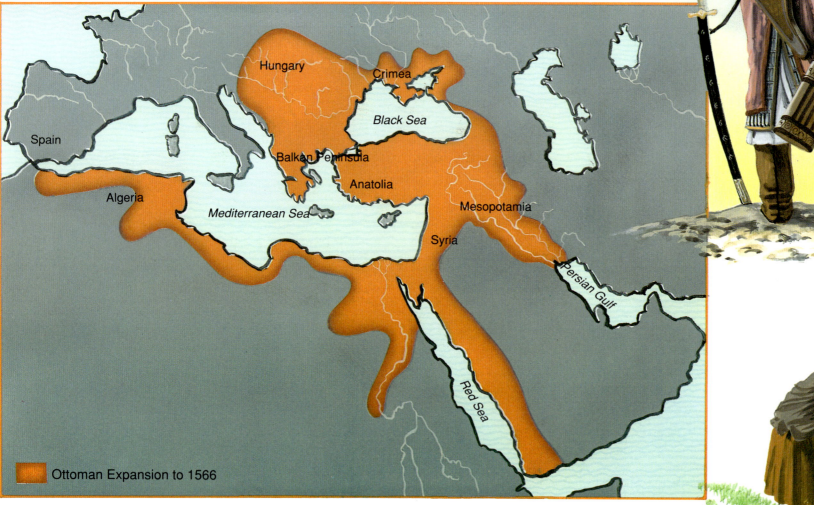

Ottoman Expansion to 1566

The conquests of Muhammad II were not limited to the Byzantine Empire. After conquering the Byzantines, the next Ottoman objective was the conquest of Serbia. However, this Balkan kingdom offered fierce resistance to the Turks and was not conquered immediately. The sultan turned back to Istanbul, consoling himself with the conquest of the cities of Sinop and Trabzon.

In 1461 Muhammad II drove the Genoese from the island of Lesbos, annexed Bosnia to his dominions, and declared war on Venice. In Asia Minor he fought and defeated the tribes of the Karamans.

A few years later the Genoese lost Kaffa in the Crimea; the Venetians lost the Ionian Islands; and the town of Otranto in southern Italy was occupied by the Turks. Trouble started with the Mamluks when the Ottomans intervened in the problems of border states located between the two powers.

In Mesopotamia the Ottomans fought against Turkish tribes seeking to gain control of Persia, Iraq, Azerbaijan, and Armenia. Uzan Hasan, one of these invading tribal chiefs, was hoping for support against the Ottomans from the Mamluks, Venetians, and Hungarians. However, the help never came, and Uzan Hasan's forces were defeated by the Ottomans.

Muhammad II was succeeded by Bayazid II, a man who loved the arts and literature more than war. He added to the architectural splendor of Istanbul but did not continue the military conquests of his predecessors. Hostilities continued with the Mamluks in Cairo. However, the Ottomans defeated and drove the Venetians out of Lepanto in 1499. This Greek seaport became an important Turkish base.

The Ottoman Empire reached its zenith of power during the 52-year reign of two sultans, Selim I and his son Suleiman. Strong internal government and renewed territorial conquest brought glory to these two great rulers.

Selim was aware of the Persian Safavid dynasty's threat to the eastern part of the Ottoman Empire. He decided to direct his efforts

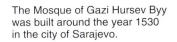
An Ottoman knight in full armor during the siege of a Balkan city

The Mosque of Gazi Hursev Byy was built around the year 1530 in the city of Sarajevo.

Below: This illustration shows a fortified monastery in Serbia early in the 15th century. The monastery is a good example of church architecture just prior to the Ottoman conquest of Serbia.

into overthrowing them. He won a great victory at Çhaldiran in 1514 and entered the city of Tabriz in northwestern Iran, taking many captives and riches. The undisciplined behavior of his janissaries obliged Selim to return to Istanbul, and the Ottoman border with the Persian kingdom was drawn near Lake Van in eastern Turkey.

Selim took Syria from the Mamluks and defeated them near Cairo in 1517. The puppet Abbasid caliph living in Cairo was taken to Istanbul where he was forced to give his blessing to the new rulers. The Ottomans took a strong stand in favor of Sunni Islam, and the Shi'ites did not hold any important public offices under the Ottomans.

Suleiman the Magnificent succeeded his father in 1520. In 1521 he took Belgrade and Rhodes, driving the Knights of St. John off the island. From 1526 onward, he controlled Hungary, and in 1529 he laid siege to Vienna, although he failed to take the city. The sultan proved to be a diplomat as well as a warrior when he made an alliance with France that helped stop Spanish influence from growing in the Mediterranean.

An untiring warrior, Suleiman again attacked the Persian Safavids. Suleiman took several of their strongholds in Azerbaijan and Kurdistan, and succeeded in annexing all of Iraq to the Ottoman Empire. The eastern Mediterranean, with the exception of the island of Malta, was entirely under the control of the Turks.

During the last years of his life, Suleiman again sought to take Vienna, which would lay open the way to the conquest of Europe. He died in 1566 while his troops were besieging the fortress of Szegedin in Hungary.

The Turkish advances in the Mediterranean were halted in 1571 by a coalition of the Vatican states, Venice, and Spain. The coalition succeeded in destroying the Ottoman fleet at the Battle of Lepanto. Within less than a year the sultan replaced the ships he lost. But the psychological damage of the defeat at Lepanto was too great, and the Turks never again threatened the western Mediterranean.

The Age of Suleiman the Magnificent

Suleiman, the greatest and most famous Ottoman sultan, had come to power under very favorable conditions. There was no internal opposition, and the military conquests of his predecessors had left him a vast empire with sufficient wealth and military power to satisfy his own political and military ambitions.

In Europe he was named "the Magnificent" for the splendor of his court. To his subjects, he was called "the Lawgiver" for his great achievements in reorganizing society and its institutions.

Suleiman concerned himself with the administration of the state. One of his first concerns was reorganizing the systems of justice and taxation to make them more efficient and effective. He also introduced a system of land surveys to enhance the collection of taxes.

Suleiman reorganized the judiciary and the bureaucracy with a network of inspectors sent from the central government to reduce corruption. He understood that effective government relied on limited interference in the actual working of government. Therefore, he introduced measures that gave considerable freedom to trusted officials.

The great jurist Ebu us-Suud Efendi was an irreplaceable adviser to the sultan in carrying out his reforms. Ebu us-Suud Efendi made a huge compilation of all Islamic laws, together with others he worked out himself, to streamline the legal system.

Suleiman drew architects and poets to his court as well as great statesmen and lawyers. He enjoyed writing poetry and sponsored the construction of mosques, bridges, aqueducts, and fortresses, which were built by the famous architect Sinan.

Suleiman also expanded the size of the empire by conquering Hungary, Libya, Algeria, Iraq, Iran, Rhodes, and a number of important islands in the Aegean Sea. Suleiman's admiral Barbarossa made the Ottomans a great naval power by defeating the Austrian Habsburg fleet in the Mediterranean and the Portuguese in the Red Sea.

The age of Suleiman was the golden age of Ottoman rule. It was a period of internal harmony and great prosperity.

A gold coin minted during the reign of Suleiman

A splendid example of calligraphy reproducing the official seal of Suleiman the Magnificent

The Social Structure

Ottoman society, like most traditional societies, divided the population of the empire into two primary categories: subjects and ruling class. Subjects were employed in the various productive activities, such as agriculture, crafts, and trade. Craftsmen had their own guilds that protected the interests of different groups. Among the ruling class were the imperial family, large estate owners, and the leaders of the military and religious institutions.

The ruling class was dominated by several institutions. At the top, of course, was the imperial Palace Institution, headed by the sultan himself. This institution included the harem, the enormous family of the sultan, with all its complicated rules and its hierarchies.

Next came the Administrative Institution, consisting of the council of ministers and the imperial treasury. The ministers and bureaucrats of this institution held the most important administrative offices of the state.

Last, was the Military Institution and the very important Religious Institution. It was their responsibility to ensure that Muslims observed religious obligations.

Suleiman held the Religious Institution in high regard. He wanted the most important wise men and scholars of Islam to teach in his great mosque in Istanbul, and he gave the necessary economic aid to foster culture and the arts.

Literature—prose, poetry and the popular compositions of itinerant troubadours—and science brought glory to the Ottoman world as they had earlier to the Abbasids. The many foreigners who traveled throughout the empire for commercial reasons brought back to Europe glowing reports of Ottoman culture and prosperity.

Left: The so-called dance of the dervishes is in reality a mystical exercise to focus concentration of the Sufi. The word *dervish* comes from an Arabic-Persian word meaning both "poor" and "dedicated to ascetic practices." The numerous confraternities of these mystics, each living under its own set of rules, were of great importance in Ottoman society.

Below: Men in characteristic Ottoman clothes in an Istanbul street. In the background are typical houses with overhanging wooden balconies. Also in the background is the mosque called Suleimaniyya, built between 1550 and 1556 by the greatest Ottoman architect Sinan on the orders of Sultan Suleiman the Magnificent.

A blue and white ceramic bowl made around 1510

The fort of Lahore, in present-day Pakistan. This imposing palace-fortress reconciles defense requirements with elegance and luxury.

A pious Indian Muslim reading the Koran

Right: Gardens were important in the expression of the Islamic decorative arts. In this Moghul painting, Sultan Babur is seen supervising the work of his gardeners. The garden is traversed by a traditional cross pattern of canals.

ISLAM IN INDIA

The Indian subcontinent, the birthplace of both Hinduism and Buddhism, has always been rich in religious life and thought. Islam entered the subcontinent when the Arabs invaded and occupied the lands that are present-day Pakistan. The conquest of north India was not simple. It was in the 8th century that the Arab armies, helped by local allies, managed to consolidate their foothold in the area of Sind, which is now western Pakistan.

Much later the Turks advanced farther into India. The Ghaznavid sultan, Mahmud, who ruled from 999 to 1030, undertook 17 expeditions into India over the course of 25 years, establishing a firm foothold in the Punjab and the region of the Ganges as far as Benares.

Mahmud was a vigorous military leader, but he was also an active supporter of culture and the arts. He was especially interested in literature and theology. He allowed the great geographer al-Biruni to follow him on his campaigns in India. Al-Biruni wrote one of his most important works about India as a result.

India was not like other regions in the Islamic Empire. Mahmud did not retain the territories he captured. India was a vast and heavily populated area from which riches could be brought back to the court of Ghaznab. At the end of the 12th century, the armies of a new dynasty from Ghor, a small state in the mountainous region of

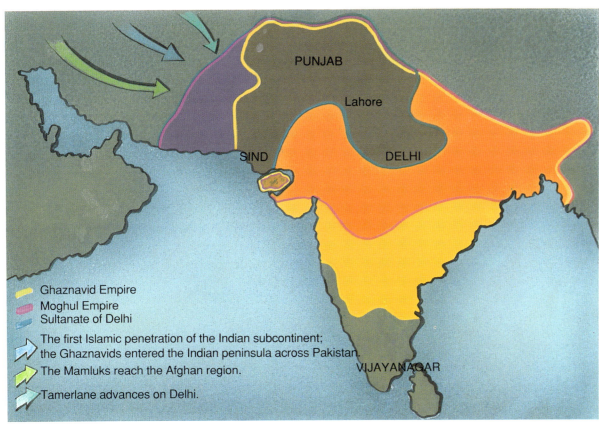

central Afghanistan, entered India. The last Ghaznavid ruler was expelled from Lahore in 1186, and new Turkish governors were installed everywhere.

Muhammad of Ghor (commonly known as Muhammad Ghori) also seized northern India and Rajasthan. In these regions Islam became the dominant religion and remained so until the 17th century.

The independent sultanate of Delhi was created in 1112, and expeditions into the south of the country began. The powerful Hindu kingdom of Vijayanagar kept its independence until the middle of the 16th century. Even after Vijayanagar capitulated to the Muslims, it retained its own religious traditions. Islam was unable to sway the local population.

The sultanate of Delhi became a kingdom of great splendor and prosperity, but it was victim to constant struggles for power between nobles in the kingdom. The ensuing state of anarchy helped speed the advance of the Mongols, who for some time had been pressing the northwest borders of India. Tamerlane invaded the subcontinent, sacked Delhi in 1398, and departed never to return.

India found itself again divided into countless kingdoms and principalities. Then a last wave of Mongol-Turkish invasions began, led by the great Babur, a descendant of Genghis Khan and Tamerlane. Babur founded the Moghul dynasty, which ruled the Indian world for two centuries. The Moghul dynasty created a sophisticated culture, with great achievements in the arts.

Indo-Muslim Art

Despite their differing conceptions of art, the Hindu and Muslim worlds did find points of contact. This was due mainly to several Muslim sovereigns who, charmed by the beauty and wealth of Indian art, encouraged a blending of the two traditions.

The main issue in blending these two great artistic traditions involved reconciling the character of Islamic art, which tends to avoid the representation of human and animal images, with Hindu art, which abounds in anthropomorphic motifs. There was also a problem of integrating Hindu and Muslim concepts of places of worship. The Hindus considered their temples the dwelling places of the divinity, while Muslims saw their mosques as places of assembly and prayer.

The first attempts to blend architecture were made in the 11th century under the Ghurid dynasty, when architects incorporated abandoned Hindu temples into new Islamic edifices. In 1194 architects began building a mosque and a minaret in Delhi with a design that followed the basics of Muslim tradition but that incorporated typically Hindu elements.

Until the advent of the Moghul Empire, the techniques and motifs of the two artistic traditions alternated according to the inclinations of those who commissioned the works of art. The Moghuls were particularly successful in blending the two traditions, and their endeavors yielded splendid monuments built in the Indo-Muslim capital of Fatehpur-Sikri.

Right: The mausoleum of Ghiyath al-Din Tughluq was built in Delhi in 1325. Its austere and majestic outer walls of red stone slope inward and are surmounted by a white marble cupola. The masterpieces of Indo-Muslim art are found especially in the architecture of tombs and fortified palaces.

A sultan riding on an elephant attended by an escort wearing typical Indian garments of white cotton

Left: Almoravid warriors ready to attack
Below: Camels carrying an African traveler to Mecca in a handsome sedan chair

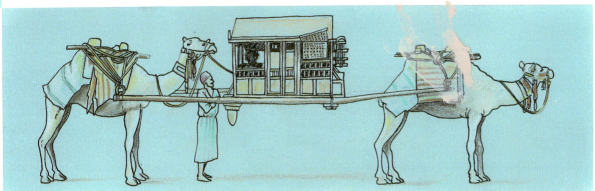

1. African warriors stand ready to oppose the advance of Islam when spread by Muslim armies.

2. The Great Mosque of Timbuktu was built in the 14th century with unbaked brick and stone in accordance with traditional architectural techniques. The mosque has all the elements found in every other mosque: the *mihrab*, the *minbar*, and the minaret, which is 52 feet tall in this case.

3. Illuminated pages of a Koran of the Hausa tribe, which converted to Islam in the 10th century

4. A rich private dwelling in Mali. The unbaked bricks are bound with mortar and covered with plaster and sand. Above the doorway is a rectangular panel surmounted by a row of small pyramids that are level with a rooftop terrace. Legend has it that this decoration was invented by an Andalusian architect who had been sent for by the king of Mali and who was able to adapt local traditions to good effect.

5. The interior portico of the Great Mosque in Kairouan, a Tunisian city of great political and religious importance in the Almoravid Age.

ISLAM IN AFRICA SOUTH OF THE SAHARA

Prior to the 12th century, it is difficult to speak in detail about the spread of Islam in Africa south of the Sahara. The little information available is from Arab manuscripts written on the accounts of travelers in the region, which may or may not be reliable.

A distinction must be made between the coasts and islands of East Africa and the great region to the south of the Sahara Desert that was known in Arabic as *bilad al-Sudan*, "the land of the blacks." The name Sudan today designates the large country south of Egypt.

Since time immemorial, the people of the African territories bordering the Indian Ocean were familiar to seafaring Arabs, Persians, and Indians. According to some traditions, the Umayyad caliph Abd al-Malik attempted to colonize the eastern coast of Africa in the 7th century.

The first centers of permanent Muslim settlements in Africa date to the 10th century. These include Mogadishu, Mombasa, Zanzibar, and settlements along the coasts of Madagascar. Most of the Muslims settling in these places were merchants. Islam also made some headway in Ethiopia, which was an ancient stronghold of Christianity in Africa. But for the most part, Islam remained confined to coastal areas of Eritrea, which were frequented by Muslim traders.

The conversion of many Africans to Islam began in a peaceful manner through the influence of missionaries and traders. However, during the period of Almoravid expansion in West Africa, the new faith was often imposed by force.

Islam spread intermittently but often did not succeed in converting the entire population of various areas. Frequently conversion to Islam was confined to certain social classes. In Ghana Islam was embraced by some inhabitants, but the king and most of the population did not relinquish their traditional religion. The situation was similar in Senegal.

However, there were many converts to Islam in the Songhai kingdom. In the 12th century the capital of this kingdom was described by the scholar al-Bakri as a rich cosmopolitan city populated by blacks, Arabs, and Berbers.

An important mosque distinguished by an unusual pyramid-shaped minaret and battlement terraces was built in the Songhai capital. The mosque followed Maghrib models of architecture, but it also initiated an authentically African Islamic architectural tradition.

Islam gained a firmer hold to the east of the Songhai kingdom in Kanem-Bornu. This firmer hold was probably due to more direct contacts there with Egypt and Tunisia. There is evidence that Kanem-Bornu sent numerous embassies to the Muslim lands along the Mediterranean. Important political figures of that country also made pilgrimages to Mecca.

Between the 12th and 14th centuries, the kingdom of Mali rose to prominence, supplanting Songhai. Islamic travelers, such as Ibn Battuta, visited and described this kingdom. Its fame also spread to the rest of the Muslim world when the kingdom's important leaders made pilgrimages to Mecca. One of these pilgrims was Mansa Musa, king of Mali from 1312 to 1337. Mansa Musa brought so much gold with him to Mecca that it caused a fall in the price of gold in the Cairo markets.

The city of Timbuktu was founded in the heart of Mali by the Berber population, or Tuaregs, in the 11th century. The city was located near the Niger River at the end of the important trade routes across the Sahara. Timbuktu became a great trading center, like a huge emporium, because of its location. It also became a center for the spread of Islamic culture in West Africa after the immigration of Arabs, who founded several important Islamic schools there.

Islam blended well into the political structures of many African societies. Islam strengthened some of them, giving new prestige to leaders and reinforcing tribal laws. This was similar to what happened in Arabia following the peninsula's conversion to Muhammad's message.

Some regions had less contact with traders and missionaries. In these regions conversion to Islam was less likely or more superficial.

Right: The decorated doorway of a modern house in Nubia (south of Egypt). Building materials and decorative motifs have remained unchanged for centuries, combining both African and Islamic elements.

To the far right is an early 16th-century minaret at Kudus on the island of Java. Javanese Muslims have always maintained a distinctive manifestation of Islam.

On the left is a 14th-century Shirazi cemetery in Zanzibar. The Shirazis were descendants of Arabs who settled in Zanzibar and married members of the local Azani tribes.

The extent of Islam in the 16th century. Muslims within both the Ottoman Empire and in independent Islamic lands retained their distinctive features and autonomous traditions but also felt themselves part of the greater world Islamic community.

THE LARGER ISLAMIC WORLD

The Ottoman Empire controlled most of the Islamic Mediterranean, but the Islamic world as a whole was much larger. Ottoman control in the west stopped at the borders with Morocco. Meanwhile, to the east, the Ottomans were never able to completely displace the Saffavids of Iran. Of course, beyond Iran lay Muslim India, Indonesia, and East Asia.

Morocco

In the 15th century, Muslims in the western Mediterranean were again attacked by Christian forces from Europe. The Portuguese controlled much of the Atlantic coast of Africa, and they were firmly established in the Mediterranean port of Ceuta in Morocco.

Morocco had frequently been independent from the dominant powers of the central Islamic lands. It had often opposed control from Islamic leaders in Baghdad or Istanbul. Under the rule of the Sherifian dynasty, Morocco achieved autonomous stature.

The Sherifians had come to power around 1525. They claimed to be descendants of both Ali and Fatima, a claim of ancestral greatness with strong appeal for the common people of the area. This claim was strengthened by the Sherifian profession of a strict interpretation of Islamic faith.

With the powerful Ottoman Empire to their east, the Atlantic to the west, and Europe to the north, the only route for Moroccan expansion was into sub-Saharan Africa. In 1590 Moroccan troops conquered Timbuktu, where they obtained great wealth in gold and slaves.

Persia

The Safavid dynasty owed its name to Shaykh Safi ad-Din, the founder of a Shi'ite religious confraternity, who died in 1334. The Safavids denied the Ottomans control over Persia. Tamerlane himself had conceded the city of Ardabil to the Safavids, and over the years their authority became political as well as religious. Internal squabbles and vicious fighting over succession within the dynasty sometimes threatened the autonomy of the region, but Saffavid power survived through the efforts of some great kings.

Shah Abbas I (1588-1629) brought the dynasty to its zenith through sound government and a well-organized army. He ceded several western provinces to the Turks in exchange for a lasting peace. As a result, he was able to devote himself to improving the administration of the kingdom and defending it from Uzbek raids in the east. Persia was a nation unto itself, and the shah was its established ruler.

India

Babur died in 1530, leaving the throne in the hands of his son. The great ruler was not a tyrant but rather an excellent ruler and a man of great culture. His memoirs contain his observations on a wide range of topics, from politics to natural science, as well as lively comments about himself and his contemporaries.

The Moghul Empire he founded derived its name from the Mongol origins of the dynasty. Babur's succession was weakened by fighting between his sons and by the attacks of Sher Shah, the master of the old Afghan kingdom, who took advantage of internal fighting in the Moghul Empire. An astute man with an excellent army, Sher Shah governed India for five years until his death in 1545.

Sher Shah's achievements were considerable. He widened roads in India, creating a vast network of highways with numerous resting places and hotels along these routes. He took harsh measures to rid the country of bandits, and he coined new money. Sher Shah concerned himself with agricultural improvements. He also ordered a census of all farming districts to ensure an efficient system of taxation based on the size of the harvest.

In 1556 Akbar the Great became the sultan of Moghul India. He was only 14 years old when he came to the throne. Akbar ended the internal rebellions, reformed the empire, and proved to be a great ruler.

Throughout his long reign, Akbar showed a genuine interest in comparative religions. He was interested in the Christian Gospels, and he made contact with Jesuit missionaries. He experimented with the idea of a new religion that would combine Christian, Hindu, and Muslim teaching and bring unity to his subjects.

Akbar's project did not succeed ultimately, but his authority was never undermined. His vast territorial conquests and his skilled exercise of power made him one of the greatest rulers of Muslim India. Akbar died in 1604.

Indonesia and East Asia

From as early as the 14th century, Indian traders journeyed far beyond the frontiers of Islam. They carried Islam to distant places, such as Ceylon, the Maldives, Burma, the Philippines, Cambodia, Java, and to the southern part of Indonesia.

Islam was soon adopted by most of the native population of Indonesia without causing any great cultural upheaval. The new converts adapted Islam to their traditions. As a result, Islam in Indonesia frequently appears very different from Islam in the Arab world. Islam allows for a great deal of regional cultural variation while preserving a solid core of unifying ideas and institutions.

Late in the 15th century and during the 16th century, Islam expanded into the Moluccas (the Spice Islands), New Guinea, and Sumatra. Northern Sumatra saw the birth of the powerful sultanate of Atjeh, which maintained diplomatic relations with the far-off Ottoman Empire itself.

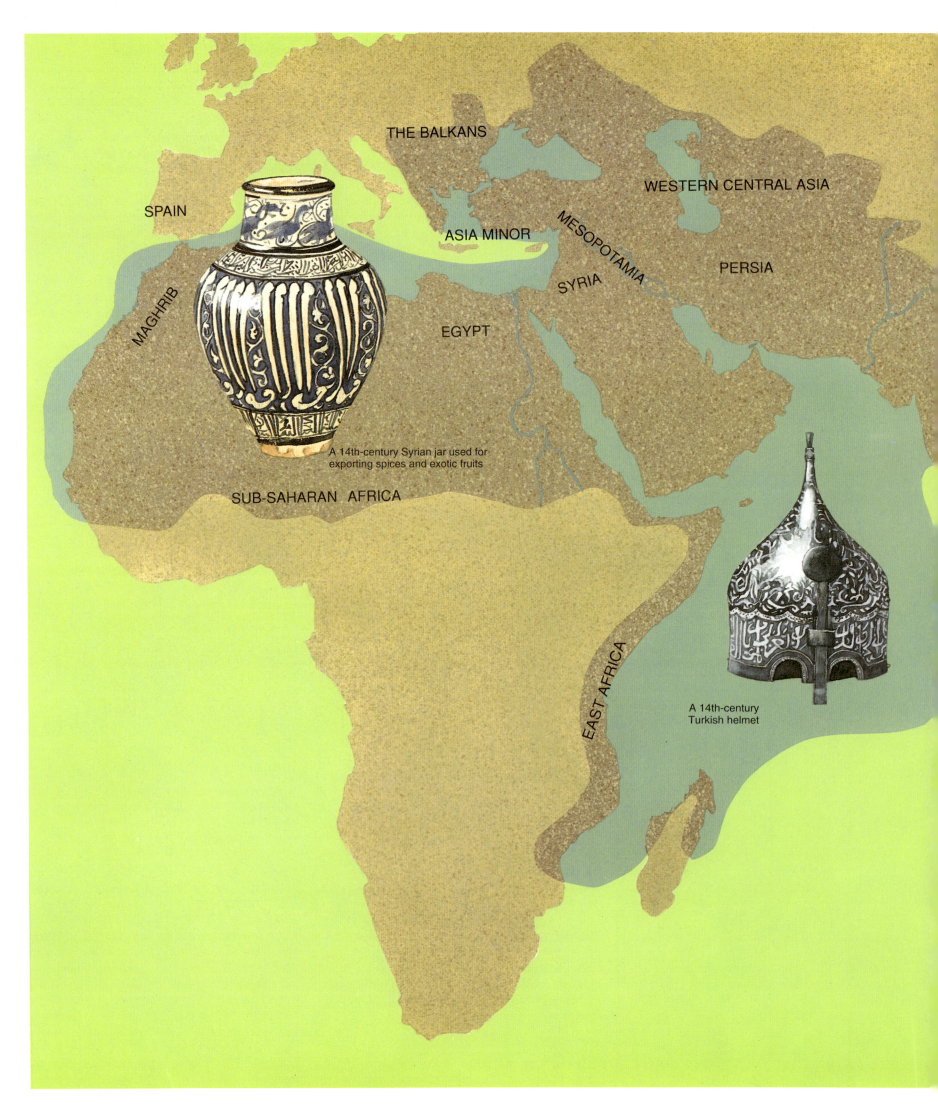

A 14th-century Syrian jar used for exporting spices and exotic fruits

A 14th-century Turkish helmet

The Extent of Islam at the End of the 16th Century

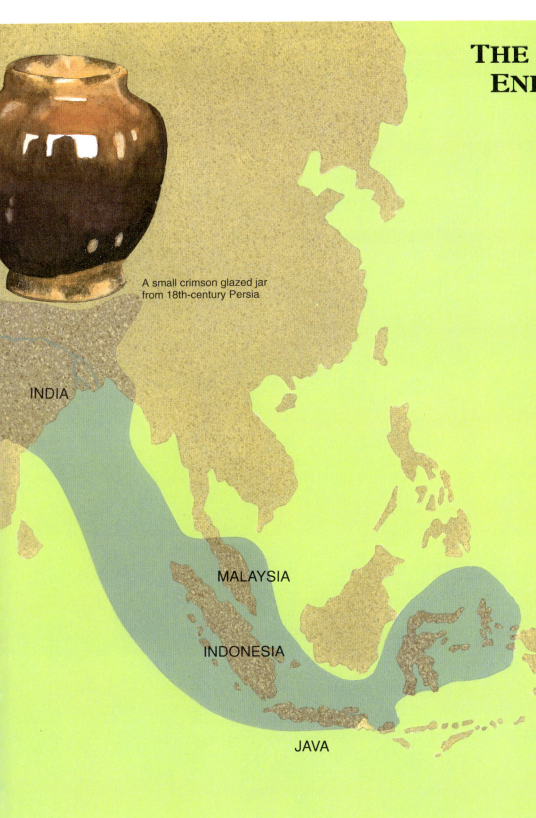

A small crimson glazed jar from 18th-century Persia

Islamic Dynasties

Listed below are the principal Muslim dynasties and the regions where they held power.

661-750 Umayyads. Syria, Arabia, Mesopotamia, Persia, western Central Asia, Egypt, the Maghrib, and Spain
750-1258 Abbasids. Mesopotamia, Arabia, Syria, Persia, western Central Asia, Egypt, the Maghrib, and Spain
756-1031 Umayyads of Spain
800-909 Aghlabids. Maghrib and Sicily
819-1005 Samanids. Central Asia and Persia
867-902 Saffarids. Persia
868-905 Tulunids. Egypt
909-1171 Fatimids. The Maghrib, Egypt, Palestine, Syria, Arabia, and Sicily
932-1056 Buyids. Persia and Mesopotamia
972-1152 Zirids. The Maghrib
977-1186 Ghaznavids. Central Asia, Persia, and northern India
11th-century kingdom of Ghana. West Africa
1056-1147 Almoravids. The Maghrib and Spain
1077-1307 The Great Seljuks. Mesopotamia, Asia Minor and northern Syria
1127-1222 Zengids. Syria
1130-1269 Almohads. The Maghrib and Spain
1169-1260 Ayyubids. Syria, Palestine, Egypt, and western Arabia
1186-1215 Ghurids. India
1230-1492 Nasrids. Spain
1250-1517 Mamluks. Egypt, Syria, Palestine, and western Arabia
14th-century Mali. West Africa
14th-century Songhai. Central Africa
1300-1924 Ottomans. Asia Minor, Balkans, Syria, Arabia, Mesopotamia, Egypt, and the Maghrib
1370-1500 Timurids. Persia and Mesopotamia
1501-1736 Safavids. Persia
1522-1903 Sultanate of Atjeh. Indonesia
1525-present day Sherifians. Morocco
1526-1858 Moghuls. India

GLOSSARY

Algorithm: Arabic, or decimal, system of numeration

Babur: Founder of the Moghul dynasty that ruled northern India for three centuries. He was a descendant of Tamerlane.

Bactriana: Ancient name of the country between the Hindu Kush mountains and the Oxus River

Bedouin: Nomadic desert tribesmen

Berbers: The indigenous peoples of North Africa

Byzantium: The name of the Roman Empire after it became Christian

Caliph: The successor of Muhammad as religious and political leader of the entire Muslim community

Caravansary: An inn surrounding a court where caravans rest at night

Confraternity: Brotherhood or society

Crusades: Military expeditions undertaken in the 11th to 13th centuries by many of the Christian powers of Europe to win back the Holy Lands from the Muslims

Damascening: Ornamentation with wavy patterns on inlaid works of precious metals

Facade: Front or face of a building

Feudalism: Form of social and military organization prevailing in Western Europe roughly from the 10th to the 16th centuries. Basic to this system was the holding of land in fief from the king, who was, in theory, the owner of all land.

Funduq: A warehouse and inn

Hadith: A record of the sayings or customs of Muhammad

Hajj: The pilgrimage to Mecca that all Muslims are expected to make at least once in their lifetime

Hammam: Public baths

Harem: The part of a house reserved for women in a Muslim household

Imam: A Muslim who leads prayers; a Muslim leader descended from Ali considered by the Shi'ites to be the divine successor of Muhammad

Ka'aba: The large cube-shaped sacred shrine of Islam, containing the black stone in the middle of the Great Mosque at Mecca

Koran: The holy book accepted by Muslims as revelations received by Muhammad from Allah

Madrassa: An Islamic school for religious studies

Mahdi: Islamic concept of a redeemer who will appear at the end of time to establish a perfect kingdom. Many reformers have laid claim to the title of Mahdi.

Mattock: A tool for digging which resembles an ax or pick

Mausoleum: A large tomb

Mihrab: Niche in a mosque indicating the direction of Mecca and prayer

Minaret: A tower attached to a mosque from which Muslims are called to prayer

Minbar: A raised platform from which the leader of prayer delivers a religious speech after the noon prayer on Fridays

Oligarchy: Government by the few

Orthodox: Conforming to established religious views or doctrine

Quraysh: A powerful Arab tribe that claimed direct descent from the Biblical Ishmael and controlled Mecca in the time of Muhammad. Muhammad was a member of this tribe.

Ramadan: The Muslim month in which the Koran was first revealed. During this holy month, all Muslims are supposed to fast from sunrise to sunset.

Ribat: A barracks that served as a fortress and a monastery

Sassanid: The pre-Islamic ruling dynasty of the Persian Empire from 226 to 637

Seljuks: The name of several Turkish dynasties that reigned in the 11th, 12th, and 13th centuries

Songhai: The Islamic African kingdom which was located in what is now Mali

Sultan: King of a Muslim state

Suq: Marketplace

Umma: The Islamic community

Visigoths: Tribes originally from the Baltic who settled in the Balkans in the 4th century. They built up an empire stretching from Gibraltar to the Loire River in present-day France. They were overcome by the Arabs in Spain early in the 8th century.

Vizier: A prime minister of a Muslim country

Ziggurat: A form of temple, which often contains a storehouse for grain

Zoroastrianism: Ancient Persian religion founded by Zoroaster, who preached that a good god and an evil god are eternally at war, though the final victor in this struggle is assured to be the good god

INDEX

A

Abbas I, 61
Abbasid dynasty, 14, 16-17, 18-19, 30, 33, 35, 36, 46-47, 53, 63
Abd al-Malik, caliph, 14, 59
Abd al-Mu'min ibn Ali, 40
Abd al-Rahman, 14, 36
Abd al-Rahman II, 36-37
Abu Bakr, 10
Abu Talib, 8
Aden, 26
Afghan region, 57
Afghanistan, 14, 42, 57
Africa
    Central, 63
    East, 27, 60
    North, 4
    south of the Sahara, 28, 58, 59-60, 61, 62
    southern, 47
    West, 27, 59, 63
Aghlabid dynasty, 38, 39, 63
agricultural production, 28-29
Ahmad. *See* Mu'izz al-Dawla
Ahmad ibn Tulun, 30
Ahwaz, 26
A'isha, 10
Akbar the Great, 61
Alawites, 13
al-Darazi, 33
Aleppo, 26, 33, 46
Alexandria, Egypt, 26, 47, 49
al-Fustat, Egypt, 14, 30
Algeria, 39, 40, 52
al-Ghazali, 19, 35
al-Hajjaj, 14
al-Hakam, 36
al-Hakim, caliph, 33
Alhambra, the, 37
al-Huqqah, 6
al-Hussayn, 12, 13
Ali, 10, 11, 12-13, 23, 25, 31, 61
Al-Jar, 26
Al-Kufa, Iraq, 4, 13, 14, 19, 20
Allah, 8, 9
al-Mahdiyya, 39
al-Mamun, caliph, 18, 20
al-Mansur, 17, 18
Almeria, 26
Almohad dynasty, 37, 39, 40-41, 63
Almoravid dynasty, 40-41, 63
al-Mu'izz, caliph, 32, 39
al-Muqaddisi, 26
al-Musta'li, 13
al-Mu'tadid, caliph, 24, 30

al-Mutasim, caliph, 18
al-Muti, caliph, 25
al-Qa'im, 34
Al-Rub al-Khali, 6
al-Walid, caliph, 11, 14
Amalfi, 26, 27
Anatolia, 5, 10, 45, 52
Ankara, 45, 49
Antioch, 33, 46
Aphrodite, 6
Arabic language, 7, 8, 27, 36
Arabs and Arabia, 5, 6-7, 12, 24, 32, 36-37, 60, 63
Aragon, 36
architecture
    African-Islamic, 59
    Aghlabid, 38
    Indo-Muslim, 57
    Islamic, 20, 39
    Mali, 59
    Mamluk, 46, 47
    Moorish, 36, 37
    Ottoman, 51
    Roman-Hellenistic, 6
    Samarra, 31
Ardabil, 26, 61
Armenians and Armenia, 14, 20, 23, 52
art
    African-Islamic, 60
    Chinese, 42
    Indo-Muslim, 57
    Islamic, 20-21, 41, 56
    Mamluk, 46, 47
artillery, Ottoman, 50, 51
Asia
    Central, 32, 34, 44, 62, 63
    East, 61
    Southeast, 27
Asia Minor, 32, 62, 63
astrolabe, 20
astronomers, 18-19
Asturias, 36
Aswan, 47
Atjeh, Sultanate of, 61, 63
Avicenna, 21, 25
Awdaghust, 26
Ayyubid dynasty, 33, 46, 63
Azerbaijan, 52, 53

B

Babur, sultan, 56, 61
Bactria, 15
Badr, 6
Baghdad, 16, 17, 18-19, 26, 28, 34, 42, 43
Bahrain, 24

Balkan Peninsula, 52
Balkans, 62, 63
Balkh, 26
Banu Hammad clan, 39
Barbarossa. *See* Khayr al-Din
Barcelona, 36
Bayazid II, 52
Baybars I, 23, 46
Bedouins, 7, 22, 39
Beijing, 43
Belgrade, 26, 52, 53
Berbers, 23, 38, 39, 41
Bet-Arsham, 6
black kite, 15
Black Sea, 52
Bou Inaniya Madrassa, 40
bow and bowmen, 22, 35, 42, 45, 49
brass, 5, 21
Brava, 26
bronze, 11, 14, 17, 20, 25, 34, 35, 37, 42, 43, 44, 47, 51
Bukhara, 14, 24, 25, 26
Burgos, 36
Bursa, Turkey, 48, 49
Buyid dynasty, 25, 34, 63
Byzantium and Byzantine Empire, 4-5, 6, 10, 14, 22-23, 27, 38, 48, 52

C

Caesarea, 6
Cairo, Egypt, 26, 46, 47, 52
calendar, Islamic, 8, 10
caliph, 10, 13
   army of, 22-23
   decline in power of, 17, 44
calligraphy, 9, 12, 20, 43, 54
camel
   caravans, 26
   domestication of, 6
Canton, 26
caravansaries, 26, 27
Carmathians, 13, 31
carpets, 20, 29, 42
Caspian Sea, 24, 25, 45
Castile, 36
Catalonia, 36
catapults, 23, 24
cavalry, 22, 23, 24
celestial globe, 20
ceramics, 4, 17, 20, 21, 26, 29, 33, 35, 43, 55
Chad, 58
China, 26, 42
Christians and Christianity, 7, 18, 33, 36, 50, 59, 61
Church of Akhtamar, 20
cities, 6, 7, 14, 19, 27, 41
city-states, Italian, 38-39
clothing, 55, 57
coin, 54
communication, 26
Constantinople, 14, 26, 48, 49, 50-51
conversion, to Islam, 26, 59
Copts, 33
Córdoba, 14, 26, 36, 37, 40
Crimea, 52
Crusaders and Crusades, 23, 32, 33, 37, 46

D

damascening, 21
Damascus, 6, 10, 11, 14, 26, 31, 32, 42, 46, 47
Daybul, 26
Delhi, sultanate of, 57
dervish, 55
dinar, 26
dirham, 26
diwans, 16-17
Druze, 13, 33
dyes, 28

E

Ebu us-Suud Efendi, 54
Edirne, 49
Egypt, 5, 6, 10, 12, 28, 30-31, 32, 33, 42, 47, 58, 62, 63
Ethiopia, 4, 59
Euphrates River, 6, 28
Europe
   Eastern, 48
   Islamic intrusion into, 37
   revival of, 27
ewer, 11

F

Fadak, 6
farming, techniques of, 28-29
Fars, 24
Fatima, 10, 12, 32, 61
Fatimid dynasty, 26, 31, 32-33, 38, 39, 46, 63
Fez, Morocco, 19, 26, 39, 40, 41
fleets, 14, 22, 23, 39, 49, 53
Franks, 4, 23
fretwork, 5, 20
funduq, 27

G

Gabriel, 8, 9
Gallipoli, 49
ganat, 29
gardens, 56
Gawar, 32
Gaza, 6
Genghis Khan, 42, 43
Genoese and Genoa, 18, 37, 38, 39, 48, 50
Gerrha, 6

Ghana, 40, 59, 63
Ghaznavid dynasty, 25, 56, 57, 63
Ghiyath al-Din Tughluq, mauseoleum of, 57
Ghor, 56, 57
Ghurid dynasty, 57, 63
glassware, 29
gold, 59, 61
government
    Abbasid, 16-17
    Almoravid, 41
    Byzantine, 10
    Ibn Tulun, 30
    Mahdi, 40
    military oligarchy, 46
    Mongol, 42, 43, 44
    Mu'awiyya, 14;
    Muslim, 10
    Nabataeans, 6
    Persian, 24
    Seljuk Turks, 35
    Suleiman, 54
Granada, 36, 37
Great Basilica, 10
Greece, 5
guilds, 28

H

Hadith, 8, 12, 20
Hadramaut, 6
hajj, 9
Hamadan, 26
hammam, 11
harem, 16, 54
Harun (al-Rashid), 18
Hassan Tower, 40
Hijaz, 6
Himyarites, 6
Hindus, 57
Homs, 26
horses, 28
Hülegü, Möngke, 42
Hungarians and Hungary, 42, 49, 52, 53

I

Ibadis, 13
Iberian Peninsula, 14, 36, 40
Ibn al-Aghlab, Ibrahim, 38
Ibn Tumart, 40
Ibn Yasin, 40
Ifriqiyya, 38, 39
imam, 8, 13
incense, 7
India, 26, 32, 44, 56-57, 60, 61, 63
Indonesia, 61, 63
Iran, 24-25, 42. *See also* Persia
Iraq, 10, 35, 52, 53

irrigation, 28
Islam
    art, 20-21
    birth of, 8-9
    cultural variations in, 61
    early conquests of, 10-11
    Five Pillars of, 8, 12
    in India, 56-57
    Iran and, 24-25
    larger world of, 61-62
    in Spain, 36-37
    in sub-Saharan Africa, 59-60
Islamic dynasties, 63
Isma'ili Fatimid dynasty, 13
Isma'ilis, 13, 31, 32
Istanbul, 48, 50-51
ivory, 5, 14, 27, 33
iwan, 20

J

Jalal al-Din ar-Rumi, 45
janissaries, 48, 49, 53
Jauf, 6
Java, 60, 63
Jerusalem, 6, 32
Jews and Judaism, 18, 33, 36
Jidda, 26
Jiroft, 25
jizya, 10

K

Ka'aba, 9, 46
Kabul, 14, 43
Kafur, 31
Kairouan, Tunisia, 26, 38, 39, 59
Kalan, 26
Kalemagdan, fortress of, 52
Kanem-Bornu, 59
Kansipur, 26
Karbala, Iraq, 12, 13
Kashgar, khanate of, 42, 44
Khadija, 8, 10
khans, 26. *See also* caravansaries
Kharijite movement, 12, 13, 14, 24
Khaya, 26
Khaybar, 6
Khayr al-Din (Barbarossa), 49, 54
Khumarawayh, 30
Khumdan, 26
Kiev, 26, 43
Konya, 42, 45
Koran, 8, 12, 20, 56
Korea, 26, 42
Kufic script, 20
Kulum, 26
Kurds and Kurdistan, 23, 24, 33, 40, 45, 53

L

Lahore, Pakistan, 56, 57
Lamu, 26
lance, 22
language
    Arabic, 7, 18, 20, 27
    Latin, 36
    Persian, 24
    translation of, 36
    Turkish, 45
Las Navas de Tolosa, 36, 37
lateen sail, 22
laws
    Ottomans compile Islamic, 54
    principles of Muslim, 8, 18
Lebanon, 33
León, 14
Lepanto, Greece, 52, 53
Lesbos, 52
Libro des Ajedres, 36
Lisbon, 36
literature
    Arabic, 14, 20
    Arabic-Christian, 36
    Indian, 56
    under Mamluk, 47
    Muslim, 19
    Ottoman, 54
    Turkish, 45
livestock, 28

M

Madagascar, 59
Madinat al-Zahra, 36
Madinat as-Salam, 17. *See also* al-Mansur
madrassa, 21, 35, 40, 42, 46
Madrassa of al-Attarin, 39
Madrassa of Sultan Hasan, 46
Maghrib, 4, 12, 14, 28, 32, 38-39, 58, 62, 63
magnetic compass, 22
Mahamud of Ghazna, 24
Mahdi, 40
Mahmud, sultan, 56
Mainz, 26
Makran, 24, 25
Malay tin, 27
Malaya, 26
Malaysia, 26, 63
Maldives, 61
Mali, 58, 59, 63
Malindi, 26
Malta, 39, 53
Mamluk dynasty, 42, 46-47, 52, 57, 63
Mansa Musa, 59

Mansura, 26
marabouts, 40
Marib, 6
markets, 27. *See also* suq
Marrakesh, 40
Marwan II, caliph, 22
mattock, 28
Mausoleum of Zubaydah, 42
mausoleums, 24, 42, 44
Mawaali, 14
Mazandaran region, Persia, 24, 25, 45
Mazara del Valo, 38
Mecca, 6, 7, 26, 32
Medina, 6, 8, 9, 11, 14, 26, 32
Mediterranean Sea, 48, 49, 61
merchants, 27, 59
Mesopotamia, 5, 12, 24, 28, 32, 34, 42, 45, 52, 62, 63
Middle East, 4, 6, 26
mihrab, 8, 30, 41, 59
minaret, 18, 20, 40, 46, 59
minbar, 8, 59
miniature paintings, 20, 29, 43
missionaries, 59
Mogadishu, 26, 59
Moghul Empire, 57, 61, 63
Mombasa, 26, 59
monastery, fortified, 53
money, 26, 44
Mongols and Mongolia, 34, 42-43, 46, 47, 49
Morocco, 4, 28, 61, 63
mosques, 14, 18, 31, 57
    'Ala al-Din, 42
    al-Aqmar, 31
    Córdoba, 37
    Damascus, 10
    Gazi Hursev Byy, 53
    Great Mosque of Mahdiyya, 39
    Green, 48
    Hassan Tower, 40
    Ibn Tulun, 31
    Kairouan, 38, 59
    Mosque of the Prophet, 8
    Samarra, 18, 19
    Songhai, 59
    Three Gates, 39
    Timbuktu, 59
    Tinmal, 41
    Tlemcen, 38
    Yusuf ibn Tashfin, 41
Mosul, 26, 34
Mozarabs, 36
Mu'awiyya, 10-11, 13, 14, 23
muezzin, 46
Muhammad
    and birth of Islam, 8-9
    conquests, 4-5
Muhammad I, 48

Muhammad II, 50, 51
Muhammad XI, 37
Muhammad Ghori, 57
Muhammad ibn Ibrahim, 20
Muhammad ibn Tughj, 31
Mu'izz al-Dawla, 25
Multan, 14
muqarnas, 20
Murad I, 49, 50
Murcia, 36
Musa ibn Nusayr, 38
music, Andalusian, 37
musk, 26
Muslim Empire, 10-11, 12-13, 18, 63
    army, 10, 22-23
    expansion of, 4-5
Musta'lis, 13
myrrh, 7
mystics, 35, 45, 55

N

Nabataeans, 6
Najd, 6
Najran, 6
Naples, 18, 26, 27
Narbonne, France, 14
Nasrids, 63
naval warfare, 23
Navarra, 36
New Guinea, 61
New Palace, 51
Neyshabur, 4, 26
Nicaea, 48
Nicomedia, 48
Niger River, 59
Nile River, 28
Nizar and Nizaris, 13
nomads, 6, 7, 14, 34, 42
noria, 28
Normans, 39
Nubia, 47, 58, 60
Nui-Lampa, 26
numeral system, Indian, 27
Nusayris, 13

O

Ogödöi, 42
oligarchy, military, 46
Oman, 6
Orhan, 48
Osman (Uthman), 48
Otranto, Italy, 52
Ottomans, 45, 46, 47, 49, 52, 60, 63
    army of, 48-49
    in Islamic world, 52-53
Oviedo, 36
Oxus River, 14, 15, 25, 34

P

Pakistan, 57
palaces, 14, 17, 37, 51, 56
Palermo, Sicily, 26, 38
Palestine, 28, 32-33, 63
Palmyra, 6
Panduranga, 26
paper, 26, 29
papyrus, 29
parchment, 29
Parthian Empire, 6
patriarchs, 50
peasants, Muslim, 28
Peking, 42
Pépin III, 14
perfumes, 27, 39
Pergamum, 48
Persia, 4, 5, 6, 10, 12, 24-25, 32, 42, 43, 44, 52, 61, 62, 63. *See also* Iran
Persian Gulf, 24, 26, 52
Petra, 6
pharmacology, 21
Philippines, 61
philosophy, Arabic, 20-21
pilgrimage, 9
Pisa, 37, 39
Plateau of Iran, 24
plow, 28
poetry, 7, 14, 20
Poitiers, France, 14
Poland, 42
ports, 26
Portuguese and Portugal, 36, 47, 61
Prague, 26
precious cloths, 26, 27
precious metals, 20
precious stones, 27
Prophet, 8, 9. *See also* Muhammad
prostration, 9
Provence, 37
Ptolemaic society, 6
Punjab, the, 56, 57
Pyrenees Mountains, 14

Q

Qasr al-Khayr al Gharbi, Syria, 11
Qasr al-Khayr al Sharqi, Syria, 11
Qaytbay, sultan, 8
Qur'an. *See* Koran
Quraysh tribe, 8, 10
Qusar Amar, Jordan, 11

R

Rabat, Morocco, 40
raids, 22, 39, 61
Rajasthan, 57

Ram, 6
Rashid ad-Din, 42
reconquest, 37, 41
Red Sea, 47, 52
reincarnation, 33
relief (wall carving), 20
religion
    combined, 61
    Mongols and, 44, 45
religious tolerance, 33, 36
Rhodes, 14, 53
ribats, 23, 39, 40
Rome, 6, 18
rudder, 22
runnel, 28
Russia, 44

S

saber, 23
saddle, 35
Safavid dynasty, 52-53, 61, 63
Saffarid dynasty, 24, 63
Safi ad-Din, shaykh, 61
Saladin, 23, 33
Samanids, 24, 25, 63
Samarkand, 14, 25, 26, 43, 44
Samarra, 18, 19, 26, 29
San'a, 6
Sanhaja, 39
Santiago, 36
sapahis, 49
Saragossa, 36
Sarajevo, 53
Sassanian dynasty, 16, 24
Sassanids, 23
scientists, 21, 54
Sea of Marmara, 51
Sebüktigin, 25
Seleucia, 6
Seleucid dynasty, 6
Selim I, sultan, 52-53
Seljuk Turks, 32, 34-35, 63
Senegal, 59
Serbs and Serbia, 48, 52
Seveners, 31
Seville, Spain, 26, 36, 37, 41
Sher Shah, 61
Sherifian dynasty, 61, 63
Shi'ites, 12-13, 14, 25, 34, 35, 40, 44, 53, 61
Shiraz, 26
Shirazis, 60
Siberia, 34
Sicily, 38, 63
siege machines, 23
Siffin, Battle of, 23
Sijilmasa, 26
silk, 26, 28
Sinai Peninsula, 31

Sinan, 55
Sinan Bey, 50
Sind, 56, 57
Sinop, 52
Sirjan, 26
Sirwah, 6
Sistan, 24, 45
slaves, 26, 27, 46, 61
Sofala, 26
Songhai kingdom, 59, 63
Sousse, Tunisia, 39
Spain, 4, 28, 32, 36-37, 38, 52, 53, 60, 62, 63
Spice Islands, 61
spices, 27
St. Sophia, church of, 50, 51
Steppes, 34, 45
Strait of Gibraltar, 4
Sudan, 59, 60
Sufis and Sufism, 19, 40, 47
Suleiman, 49, 52, 53, 54-55
sultan, 35, 46, 57
Sumatra, 61
sunna (path), 12
Sunnis, 12-13, 14, 20, 33, 34, 35, 40, 42, 44, 46, 53
suq, 27, 28
suras, 8
Syracuse, Sicily, 38
Syria, 4, 5, 6, 10, 28, 31, 32, 33, 42, 52, 53, 62, 63
Szegedin, 53

T

Tabriz, Iran, 42, 53
Tabuk, 6
Taif, 6
Tamerlane, 44-45, 48, 57, 61
Tariq ibn Ziad, 14, 15
taxation, 10, 14, 18, 28, 41, 44, 54, 61
Tayma, 6
temple, Hindu, 57
Temple of Baal (Palmyra), 6
Temple of Jupiter, 10
Temujin, 42. *See also* Genghis Khan
textiles, 26, 27, 28
Thamud, 6
Theodosius, emperor, 10
Thousand and One Nights, A, 18
Tibet, 26, 34
Tigris River, 17, 28
Timbuktu, 59, 61
Timurids, 63
Tinmal, Morocco, 41
Tlemcen, Algeria, 38, 41
Toghril Beg, 25, 34, 35
Toledo, 36, 37
Topkapi, 51
Torre de Oro, 41

Trabzon, 52
trade, traders, and trade routes, 6, 26-27, 46, 47, 59, 61
Trajan, emperor, 6
Transoxiana, 5, 14, 25, 45
Traret, 26
tribes and tribesmen, 22
tribute, 49
Tripoli, Libya, 14, 39, 46
troubadours, 37
Tuaregs, 59
Tulunids, 30, 63
Tunis, 26
Tunisia, 32
Turkestan, 26
Turkmenistan, 27
Turks, 14, 34-35, 40, 45. *See also* Seljuk Turks
Twelvers, 13, 31

U

Ukhaidir, 17, 19
ulama, 21, 30
'Umar (Omar), 10, 22, 24
Umar II, caliph, 14
Umayyad dynasty, 10, 14-15, 36-37, 38, 63
umma, 11, 12
uniforms, military, 31, 48, 53, 62
Universal History, The (Rashid ad-Din), 42
'Uthman, caliph, 8, 10, 23
Uzan, Hasan, 52
Uzbeks, 61

V

Valencia, 36
Van, Lake, 42, 53
Vandals, 36
Vardun, 26
Vatican states, 53
Venetians and Venice, 18, 26, 27, 38, 48, 50, 52, 53
viceroys, 30

Vienna, 53
Vijayanagar, 57
vizier, 16, 25
Volga River, 42

W

warfare
    Islamic, 4-5, 22-23
    Mongols, 42, 48
    Ottoman, 48-49, 50
    Turkish, 35
warriors
    list of, 22
    types of, 23
Wasit, Iraq, 14
water, as precious commodity, 41
waterwheel, 28
weapons, 14, 26
wood carvings, 30

X

Xerxes, 24

Y

Yamama, 6
Ya'qub ibn Layth al-Saffar, 24
Yathrib, 6, 8
Yazid, caliph, 12, 13
Yemen, 5, 6, 7, 12

Z

Zabid, 26
Zafar, 6
Zanzibar, 26, 59, 60
Zayd and Zaydis, 8, 12, 13
Zenaga, 39
Zengids, 34, 63
Zenobia, Queen (Palmyrene), 7
ziggurats, 19
Zirids, 39, 63
Zoroastrianism, 13, 25